On The Plant Floor

A practical guide to daily leadership in the manufacturing factory

BRYAN D GEARY
CARLTON F SORRELL

ISBN: 1477697888
ISBN 13: 9781477697887

Table of Contents

About the Author

Lived As Well As Written

OPF Enterprises, LLC
PO Box 16898
Missoula, MT 59808
Phone = 406-493-1102

Email = bryan@ontheplantfloor.com
        carl@ontheplantfloor.com
Website: http://www.ontheplantfloor.com

Carl on Bryan Geary

Bryan has over 22 years of experience in different manufacturing roles including production operator, laboratory technician, laboratory manager, production supervisor, production manager, assistant plant manager, plant manager, and director of manufacturing. He is a true example of someone who gets his foot in a door and ends up directing the whole shooting match. And I mean this in the best possible way. He is just that good.

Bryan has told you how he and I met and I can add that in our very first meeting, I gave the standard, "Now I don't want to hear what you *think* I want to hear, I want you to tell me what you really think!" The vice-president of manufacturing, Mr. Bill Hanks, was present at this meeting and doubled over with laughter. He managed to get out "Carl that is the LAST thing you need to worry about!" And so it was. Bryan always gave me his best advice even when it was as simple as instructing me to get my head out of my butt.

Bryan is whip-smart and a true renaissance man. In addition to being an accomplished musician, he can out-geek most I.T. guys in his spare time. There is very little Bryan hasn't been able to learn, and like most great learners, he is also a great teacher. His dedication to manufacturing is second to none and I have learned a very great deal from him. He and I are fast friends even though we have highly dissimilar personalities. I have always believed that a person is successful if he has five friends he can truly count on. By that measure, I am successful and Bryan heads that list of five, and I am proud for him to be there.

For the reader, we hope you get the best of each of us, and that the sum of our collaboration is greater than the sum of our individual talents.

Bryan on Carl Sorrell

Carl has 35 years of experience in various manufacturing roles including production operator, front line supervisor, engineering manager, maintenance manager, production manager, plant manager, director of research and development, and vice president of manufacturing. He claims to be an engineer and can produce a Bachelor of Science diploma in Ceramic Engineering from the University of Missouri-Rolla (now Missouri Science and Technology).

Carl and I met in Jackson, Tennessee, when he arrived at a factory where I had worked for several years. After turning down a promotion to plant manager, I remained assistant plant manager when Carl was brought in from outside the company.

He had, and sometimes still does have, a cowboy-style approach to leadership that engages battles head-on and drives improvements with a forceful spur in the rear as needed. Gentle he often is not. As a result of this style, I did not take well to his leadership and initially became insulted by many of his actions. I believed he showed no consideration for my dedication to the plant, or any concern for the people – many of whom were proud of their long service.

Nevertheless, over a relatively short period of time, Carl and I began a good working relationship. Together we fought the daily battles of manufacturing while finding the good in each other.

Quite often in this book you will read situational descriptions and recognize that these were actual problems that we worked on as a team. I would not have believed those many years ago that Carl and I would be working together today. Even now there are people who don't know if we are dedicated friends, adversaries, or just two guys playing good cop – bad cop. What we share is a deep commitment to manufacturing and a true love for the plants and people we have met during our journey. These people on the plant floor have taught us much about how to improve operations, but more importantly, they have taught us how to improve ourselves.

Carl has been a great leader, mentor, advisor and most of all a friend to me for several years. It is often said that you shouldn't get too close to people in the working world or your judgment will be clouded. I'm thankful that I did not accept that belief. I would have missed out on a great, lifelong friendship that has helped me win many battles on and off the plant floor.

Testimonials

To the new readers!

The authors, Carl Sorrell and Bryan Geary, have spent years on the "Plant Floor", and the pages of this book will give you insight into the means and methods that will help you or your organization improve the process and thus the bottom line of your company. These two men worked with me for many years with Dal-Tile Corporation which is the largest manufacturer and seller of ceramic tile in the USA and in the top ten in the world. Both Carl and Bryan were instrumental in leading process improvement and management of different production facilities and understand how to set goals, outline objectives, and design the "how to" to achieve the goals. Additionally, they understand how to translate the corporate or higher level yearly objectives into daily "on the floor" performance goals that lead individuals and departments to reach out to achieve the company targets. The translation of the company goals into understandable and workable daily process targets is one of the more challenging tasks of a floor manager, and the authors have learned and taught this discipline on many levels of the manufacturing organization.

The book is entertaining while educating, and we have learned that the "plant floor" can achieve higher results when the people understand the process, buy into not only the success but own any failures. If you have worked or will work in manufacturing, you will learn that process variables are many, and the proper control of all the variables will determine the end results. Carl Sorrell and Bryan Geary worked hands "On the Plant Floor", and they have brought to you examples and methods to improve your performance! Good Reading and Good Luck!

Bill Hanks
Chief Executive Officer
Rosebriar Holdings Corporation

I met Carl in the early nineties, he helped me open a plant in south east Idaho. At that time, Carl was without a doubt a "God-send." I met Bryan a few years later and we all spent a few days fly fishing on a river in south east Idaho. You have no better opportunity to learn what a man is really like than time spent in close quarters on a jet boat. Since then I have had the pleasure to read their book on managing from the plant floor. There is absolutely no doubt that this presentation is the best of its kind that I have read. Coaches and managers of successful teams are on the field, not in the club houses or sky boxes. It will absolutely amaze you how many times you are lured away from your plant floor if you allow it to happen. Carl and Bryan have years of experience doing plant management from the floor. The two of them have really gone into great detail to give you a guide to operate your plant at a profit. Good luck to you and to them in your future quest.

Earl Mann
Friend and retired plant manager

I first met Carl in 1984. He was the General Manager of a plant under construction that I had a strong part in designing from Italy. Carl was the brain of putting together the best group of people in the ceramic tile industry in the early 80's. This was my first trip to the United States and I was very impressed to find Carl and his team. He and I took the very best of both the American and European culture and methods to build and operate a world class plant. I met Bryan a few years later after I had been appointed the Vice-President for the same company that owned the plant Carl and I built.

Both Carl and Bryan have spent many years working "on the plant floor" and this book reflects their knowledge, beliefs, and ethics. Their book is like a concentrate of the half a century plus years of combined experience. If you follow the guidelines clearly layed out for you in these chapters you will find ways to become a better leader, manager, and team member. Carl and Bryan live and breathe manufacturing and this book will help you to reach your goals and, just maybe, discourage you from re-inventing the wheel!

Silver Cornia
CTO The Tile Doctor

Preface

Why would anyone be crazy enough to write a practical guide for people working in an economic sector of the American economy-manufacturing-that is rapidly dying? Manufacturing ain't dying. So now that question is put to rest..... oh, it isn't you say? Here are a few statistics.

In 2007 the industrial output of the United States was $2.69 trillion dollars, larger than the industrial output of China, India and Brazil combined. From 2000 to 2006 the industrial output of the United States has remained virtually unchanged.

These statistics notwithstanding, manufacturing has been undergoing a massive change in the past twenty-five years. One in six manufacturing jobs since 2000 has disappeared. That trend is likely to continue as long as manual labor intensive jobs are sent overseas where companies can take advantage of lower cost labor. These jobs are not likely to come back as America ceded them to third world companies. This happened in exactly the same manner and for the same reasons as the Industrial Northeast textile mills who moved their production to the American South in the mid twentieth century. Beginning in the late 1970's, this production was again moved to Mexico to take advantage of lower labor cost. Ironically, this production has largely been moved to Asia in just the last ten years as China opened their industrial doors with the lowest labor costs in the world.

Yet America remains the world's largest manufacturer with the highest productivity in the world. What has changed are the products being produced. From airplanes, to chemicals, to food, America leads the world in manufacturing. America's products consumed in the United States are not as easily recognizable as they were formerly, especially if you shop at Wal-Mart or Target. Yet that Toyota you drive is probably made in Kentucky, Texas or Indiana, and the Honda your spouse drives is likely made in Alabama or Ohio. The ownership of these companies may not be American, but the manufacturing surely is.

But we haven't yet told you why we wrote a book titled "On The Plant Floor". The simple answer is that after a combined 50+ years of hands-on manufacturing experience we have a simple goal:

- *Provide a practical reference book for plant people that can help guide supervisors and managers to better decisions.*

To our knowledge nothing like this exists in the market. When we look back at our careers, we recognize that while there are plenty of business books and technical books that provide some good information, there is no real "how-to" book.

You will recognize many terms we use again and again: *culture, engagement, disclosure, entitlements, failure, and humility.* These terms form our core belief system developed from years of collaboration with the many fine folks we have met along our way. Leading, being led, teaching, learning, being managed, watching others fail, and experiencing our own failures (with a few victories) have all been a part of our journey to On *The Plant Floor.*

You will understand that everything rises and falls on leadership, and the leadership is you and your team. The leadership team spends most of their time (as it should be) On *The Plant Floor* with the operators, equipment, maintenance personnel, and your suppliers; learning the process, making improvements, and evaluating your core team members. You are charged with creating a culture of high engagement from everyone in the plant.

You will see that you are the company to your subordinates and it is critical to infuse the team with the understanding that high standards – whether for productivity, quality, or safety – must be the norm rather than the exception.

We have often experienced and believe that being a front line supervisor is tough and demanding. In fact, nobody above the level of front line supervision directly contributes to the profitability of an operation. To those of you with the fortitude to do this work day in and day out, we take our hats off to you.

This book is also directed to those in what we believe to be the most difficult job in all of manufacturing – plant manager. We both have held this role in a number of plants and speak from lessons learned as well as lessons earned. It is the plant manager to whom it falls to bear the cross of *everything rises and falls on leadership.* The plant manager is the leader who is largely responsible for the culture, awareness, and passion needed to drive a plant, while at the same time, remains calm and thoughtful enough to inspire confidence. It is not a job for the weak or weary, nor is it a job for those with superman complexes, white knight mentalities, pessimistic demeanors, or those with an inability to make decisions.

We will address the fallacies of the *magic wand and the secret button*. Rather, we will show you (and show you how to show others) that progress and improvement are the results of incremental adjustments and changes that are suggested and implemented by many different people.

If you are to be a great plant manager, you will fill several roles including coach, mentor, father, brother, friend, counselor, cheer leader, and disciplinarian. Most of all you will learn that the ability to successfully *manage both upstream and downstream* in your organization is the most important skill you can have.

It has been our pleasure over many years to spend our careers among the wonderful folks who go to work every day and make things. In our humble opinion, it is a high calling and one that only special people can answer.

Welcome to Management...Now What?

For The New Supervisor

A ringing telephone brings you out of a deep sleep. You can barely read the clock on the nightstand but sure enough, it says 3:17 AM. It must be bad news; nobody calls at this time of night with good news. Hesitating, you scramble for the phone and answer. "Hello, hello, hello?" "Hi, Mr. Smith, sorry to call so late, but this is George out at the furnace. We have a problem and they told me you were the new guy in charge. WELCOME TO MANAGEMENT!

You have been superbly trained for your new position and....pardon me? You say you haven't been trained? Oh! Any training you received was in the gee-gaw pressing process ....the nuts and bolts of how the machines operate and suchlike? I see. You mean that NOBODY taught you how to manage? Shocking. But you are lucky. You were the best machine operator in the gee-gaw pressing

1

department for five years and know the machines backward and forward so you will have no problem in....sorry, what was that? Oh, I understand....it's a lot different when running the entire gee-gaw department. You paid a lot of attention to your supervisors but now you are finding that what you thought was good (or bad) as an operator is not so clear-cut. No matter, you graduated summa cum laude from a prestigious college with your all-purpose engineering degree and your mastery is assured.....excuse me? They didn't teach gee-gaw pressing at your school? H'mmmmmm. Let's run for the hills!

Of course your situation probably isn't all that dramatic, but as the newest management member in your plant, you are certainly dealing with the hope and promise of your new position as well as the uncertainty of entering new territory. Keep in mind that you are not alone. You were appointed to your new position by people who believed you were qualified for the position and want you to succeed. It's either that or your daddy is a company VP. No matter how you got here, you're here.

You will often read in this book our preference for calling operational segments of a plant "sequences" rather than by the more traditional "departments." Among the reasons for this is that "departments" is not an accurate description for the processes in a manufacturing plant. The very simple diagram below can be used – on a very high level – to describe any sequence in a factory.

All manufacturing sequences involve taking materials and information, making changes to them, and passing the altered product to another sequence or to the final customer if your operation (shipping) is the last sequence in the chain. Now "department" doesn't really describe this process, does it? Our terminology is important because _the most important thing you must learn upon moving into management is that you are, for the first time in your career, part of a team._ How can that be? We've been told over and over that we are "part of a team" and that "teamwork" is the key to success whether we are machine operators or janitors.

We submit to you that the success of a janitor is largely dependent on individual effort; while successful supervision is possible only when the sequences, and those who run them, are continually engaged with each other to ensure smooth operation.

We perfectly understand that many of you are sick unto death when you hear someone utter the word "TEAMWORK" usually punctuated with an EXCLAMATION POINT! Sometimes you even get three of 'em !!! The entire working world seems to be obsessed with TEAMWORK! The reason for this is pretty simple: when teamwork is real, it works.

Neither of your humble authors are rah-rah kind of factory guys who lead "THE TEAM" in daily cheers. Cheers and "morale building" exercises generally don't work as intended and sometimes can even retard progress. The teamwork we believe in can be described as "enlightened self-interest." Look again at our simple chart. You are taking materials and information from a sequence, processing them, and moving them on in an altered form to another sequence. Those sequences are supervised by someone just like you, and the success of your sequence is dependent on them to properly deliver to, and take from, your sequence. Simply put, your success is in the hands of others. It is in your best _self-interest_ to be engaged with them. When you have a group of individuals enlightened in the knowledge that their success depends on others, then you have a team.

Manufacturing is Football

We love sports and we love baseball and football most of all. There is nothing like the crack of a bat during a World Series game or a leaping touchdown reception during the Super Bowl. And while both are team sports we love, we have come to realize that the special world of manufacturing is a lot more like football than baseball.

Consider the exquisitely crafted game of baseball. One man who stands in the batter box and stares down a pitcher and eight other men who try to stop him from hitting the ball. One man against many - one _individual_ man. Another way to look at the game is that the real reason there are eight defensive fielders out there is simply to hold down the damage if the pitcher screws up. After all, if the pitcher strikes out 27 men in a row, then there is no need for an infield or outfield. Well, you would need a catcher, but only because otherwise the home plate umpire is gonna have a bad day! And if the pitcher does serve up a home run to a batter, it might be just that one hit that wins the game....what the heck did the team need the other 8 batters for? Simply put, the magnificent game of baseball is a collection of individual efforts.

Football is also dependent on individual efforts, but those efforts are dependent on the efforts of each team member every time the ball is snapped. If just one offensive lineman fails in his duties, the quarterback is sacked by the defense – and if somehow the quarterback evades the rush long enough to get a pass off, it will come to nothing if a receiver is not there to catch the ball. Individual accomplishments are less important in the game of football than the teamwork between players.

And so it is with the manufacturing management team. Your team can only be successful if each and every supervisor does his job so that the output of his sequence, materials and information is within specification for quantity and quality. It won't do any good for one sequence to hit a home run while other sequences are striking out. If you all learn to block and tackle like a football team, you will give yourselves the best chance for success. Your sense of enlightened self-interest will also lead you to understand that some team members are weaker than others in some areas and will need extra help. A football kicker is usually a terrible tackler, but he plays an important part on the field. You will have kickers on your management team as well.

As a new supervisor, you will be called rookie more times than you care for, but wear the label with pride for it shows you are on the team. The lessons you learn (or don't learn) in this early stage of your career will have a major influence on the rest of it. All rookies are not created equal.

- No experience: The lowest level of rookie supervisor includes new college graduates (don't argue!) and others with no supervisory or process experience. It's relatively rare that someone without any experience and no diploma to be hired as a supervisor and all _too_ common for the newly minted college graduate. New college graduates are NOT dumb, just ignorant in the sense that they have no practical application experience. Ignorance is curable and college graduates usually learn pretty quickly.

- Plant Experience: This next level applies to those promoted from the hourly ranks but with no experience in the sequence they now supervise. We heartily agree with a promote-from-within policy, and many firms using this method make it a policy that a new supervisor is assigned to a new department. This avoids problems with supervising former co-workers at the cost of operational expertise.

- Experience with another company: This is a highly populated category in rookie-dom. If Bubba supervised the gee-gaw pressing sequence for XYZ Corporation he is a likely candidate to supervise gee-gaw pressing in your plant.

- Technical experience: This highest level on the rookie ladder has been promoted from the ranks and has sequence experience in your plant or from another plant in your company. He might also have technical experience (think quality auditor) that has seen the overall operation and has a good sense of the inputs and outputs of each sequence.

Your actions and performance will in part be judged by where you fit in this ranking. You might also get a bit more leeway and freedom if you are sequence experienced within your company than you would if you are a (ignorant but not dumb) new graduate.

Carl –

During the planning phase in a start-up company, Bryan and I hired a summer intern to help us out with the scale-up of R&D processes to full scale manufacturing. Jeremy stayed with us for twelve weeks and often travelled with either of us to manufacturers' test sites. He probably got to see more than a typical intern would see and we ran him pretty hard through the process. We were pleased with his performance and as he was preparing to return to college for his junior year of Ceramic Engineering training at Missouri Science and Technology, we asked him to sit down and write a summary of what he learned during his time with us. He listed at least twenty-five items, but the most important item was "I learned I didn't know anywhere near as much as I thought I did." Smart kid.

Despite where you fit in the hierarchy, we can offer you some practical guidelines to help you in your new position derived from our experience. We remember all too well what it was like to be a rookie.

Listen more than you speak. You're new, and those around you, including your subordinates, are not. Most likely, the old hands will be willing to help a rookie learn his new job if that rookie doesn't suffer from diarrhea of the mouth. This doesn't mean you can't join in the lunch conversation about how pathetically the Dallas Cowboys have been playing, but when the discussions get serious, develop a sudden and mild case of laryngitis.

Be cautious when offering your opinion about anyone else in the company. Rookie opinions can be seen as arrogant, and if heard by the wrong people, can hurt your team and your career. The culture of your plant *should* guarantee that rookies are respected and that they have a voice – so use it wisely. After a few ill-considered comments, your more experienced team members might beat you about the head and shoulders to a point where you might learn something. And it is always possible that the something might be you don't want to remain in management.

Carl –

Early in my career I was an ignorant rookie and I opined to a visiting divisional personnel director that our VP was an idiot. Two days later my plant manager called me into his office to ask me how in hell I could have been so stupid. Not only was I stupid in my judgment, but I was actually naïve enough to believe my conversation with the personnel guy was confidential....after all, he told me it was! My blunder almost cost me a promotion and would have if my plant manager had not intervened, spreading oil on the waters. Thanks, Walt.

Pay attention not only to the good things happening around you, but also to the bad things. You will learn more about leadership by understanding the mistakes of others than you will by studying the good decisions. Mistakes cause exceptions, which in turn, cause the team to correct them. When mistakes are made, you get to see multiple actions and how they play out. The old hand who appears to *never* make mistakes learned plenty by watching others' mistakes as well as making a few of his own when he was cutting his teeth.

Be humble. This goes hand in hand with not talking too much. You might have graduated summa cum laude from Enormous University but nobody cares. Your team members want to know if you will spend a night working with them underneath a press, not if you can solve quadratic equations. Reaching for a wrench will earn you a lot more respect than reaching for your scientific calculator.

Understand you *will make mistakes.* Try not to beat yourself up over them (others will do that for you) and work to learn from them. Above all, do not blame your mistakes on anyone but yourself. "I screwed up" is among the better things you can say and is certainly better than trying to evade responsibility. "I screwed up but I won't do it again" is even a better thing to say. Do your best to make mistakes of commission rather than mistakes of omission. You will go a long way in your learning when you understand that making bad decisions is preferable to not making decisions at all announcing to your team you are weak and/or lazy. One final word about your mistakes, never, ever, try to cover them up. It is much better to fall on your own sword than for your concealed mistakes to place the sword in the hands of your boss.

One of the more difficult things you will face is simply how to act around your subordinates. In the blink of an eye, seemingly, you are expected to be their priest, coach, disciplinarian, and to honorably represent your management team. This is especially true for the lowest ranking rookie who may never have stepped foot in a manufacturing plant. The top three rookie classes at least have the advantage of having been supervised in the manufacturing world and have role models – good or bad. Most larger companies will have you sit in a multi-hour training course designed to keep you and the company out of trouble. Such courses will cover the dos and don'ts of racial, religious, and sexual harassment/discrimination. You must pay attention and absorb this training, but know that like any training course, it will touch just the basics of how to act. And what are you to do if there is not even this basic training?

The Mentor

Mentoring has been around forever, and before it was called mentoring, it was known as apprenticeship-the training a novice went through before they could become journeymen. The apprenticeship training paired a master craftsman with a novice, and over a period of years, the old master imparted his techniques, tricks and shortcuts as well as his wisdom to the apprentice. The industrial revolution largely put an end to this tradition which today is practiced only in the highly skilled trades, usually under a union regimen. Happily, for us, mentoring is alive and well in the manufacturing world. Good thing, too, because a good mentor is invaluable to your growth.

Both of us have been fortunate enough to have been mentored, and both of us have been honored by being able to mentor others. Now unless you work for a company that has a structured mentoring program (and that's unlikely in a manufacturing plant), you are faced with:

a. Actually realizing you need a mentor.
b. Finding one.

7

Fortunately, you have read this chapter and by now realize you need a mentor. So all you are left with is finding one. That is also relatively easy - you work with him. He might be sitting at the desk to your right, or you might find him in your boss's office – that's right, your boss. Your mentor should possess both the temperament to help people and a willingness to do so. Many people have one or the other quality but fewer have both in equal measure. Your mentor will probably be one of the calmer personalities in your work world. He will be the guy who will listen to all opinions until it is time to make a decision. And he'll make those decisions with little hesitation and no self doubt. He'll be the guy who rarely is impulsive or rash. Most importantly, he is likely to be one of the guys who spend significant time On The Plant Floor. If promotions have removed him from the plant floor, he will spend time griping about it.

Find this guy and tell him you need his advice on how to lead people and improving production performance because you want to do a good job. If *you* believe your words, he will too. And he will know better than you that asking for his help does not show your weakness, but that you understand there is no substitute for experience.

This won't be the last time we write about the special issues facing a new supervisor. You will find situational references to new managers throughout the book, but the following chapters will be of special interest to rookies.

2. Not Everybody is Like You – So What!

3. If You Don't Care, Why Should They?

5. You manage things but you lead people

7. The Walk

12. Emails are Evil

16. Building the Culture

17. Celebrate Victories Large and Small

21. In or Out of the Organization

23. Staying Humble

24. The Balance

So read on and go conquer the world! We have your back.

Not Everybody Is Like You – So What!

That's why they sell blue cars and white cars.

The title of this chapter states the obvious, right? *Of course* not everybody is like you. Some are taller, shorter, thinner, fatter, a different sex, ad infinitum. You already know this! Before you judge us to be captains of the obvious, let us dive just a bit deeper and show you how the obvious is anything but. We will cover plant culture in Chapter 16) Building The Culture, but here we want you to be aware of the impact your decisions and actions will have on others. We also want you to maintain your sanity.

Your job is to make a profit. You do this by managing your plant or sequence to produce products which the company sells and makes money. You operate to a budget that targets costs for materials, energy, overhead, and labor. Within reasonable limits, materials, energy, and overhead are pretty much fixed. Planned labor headcount is also fixed; one operator per two machines, three forklift drivers per line, and so forth. So if all these things are constant, why do you have so much variation in your operation? Why are you spending so much time trying to figure out why #2 line is producing one-half the output with twice the rejects compared to the identical #4 line? After many days of direct observation, researching the equipment downtime logs (you have those, right?), and conferring with mechanics, you come to the conclusion that the difference between #2 line and #4 line is the people running them. They just aren't getting the job done. Why?

Since you are a conscientious manager you schedule one-on-one meetings with the people operating the line to get their opinions. To each of them you say:

"The line you run is having some serious productivity issues and is running just half the output of #4 line while your reject rate is twice as high. Can you shed some light on this problem?"

The answers go something like this:

- Mary: "I don't have any idea. Nobody told me this was happening. That's the problem around here – no communication!"

- Bill: "Of course I can tell you. The line #4 operators are a bunch of brown-nosers and they always get to run the easy stuff!"

- Steve: "You know, boss, I have been concerned about this for some time. I would really like to get the bottom of it as well. I think our crew could use a little more training – maybe the line #4 operators know some tricks that we haven't caught on to yet."

- Brenda: "I'm trying my best but the equipment just doesn't want to cooperate. My life would be a lot easier if things ran better."

- Lonny: "Why are you asking me? I thought it was your job to figure this stuff out. I sure as hell do my job every day!"

- Willie: "You just watch the maintenance crews once in a while. They are always hanging around #4 line to talk to that pretty gal running their gee-gaw press. If we had that much attention, we would run the pants off them."

Wow. Six different people give you six different answers to the exact same question. Your data supported conclusions must be wrong! After all, your people who are right there on the line every day are giving you all kinds of answers you didn't expect. Some of these folks were defensive to the point of hostility; some were asking for help, and only Steve gave you the answer you were looking for. Since one out of six isn't a good percentage, you decide that valid data must be gathered, more opinions sought, and more time taken to reach a conclusion.

Tick – Tock… tick – tock… tick- tock.

You've fallen into the trap.

Carl –

The best advice that I ever got was from my first boss. He told me "Carl, you can't expect everyone to react to things as you do. Not everybody is like you."

In the example of the differences in line productivity, we see that six people gave six different reactions to the same question. Expect this more often than not. Why? They are six different people who have different parents, childhoods, education, and experiences. They are *individuals who are different than you.* The point drawn here is a simple one: *If you spend all your time worrying about what people think, you will not be able to lead them because you will be incapable of making decisions.* After reading that sentence you might be asking yourself whether this means you are condemned to be a jack-booted tyrant, imposing your will on an ungrateful workforce. The answer is "No!" because the corollary to the first point is this: *Given the opportunity, most people want to do well.* The point and corollary are two sides of the same coin and one you want to always have in your pocket. Nobody goes into a job wanting to fail. Whether their motivation is climbing the ladder, waiting for a better opportunity elsewhere, or simply putting food on the table, they want to succeed and your job is to give them that opportunity.

Armed with this knowledge, you can stop worrying so much about the six different reactions to your productivity question and place faith in your carefully gathered data and conclusions. You decide to take the line #2 operators, one at a time, and pair them up with their counterpart on line #4 for a few days. Lo and behold, Steve was right. There were some tricks that the line #4 operators knew. Still, the big difference was, as you suspected, training. Line #2 productivity begins to rise and the operators are mostly smiling when you walk the line. Still, they are not quite there yet. If Steve was right, maybe Brenda had a point about the equipment "just not running right." You decide to let the line #4 operators spend some time on line #2. After a couple of shifts they point out to the maintenance crew some minor sprocket wear and some machine setting differences. (By the way, Willie was right about the maintenance crew hanging out on the other line that Suzie sweet-talked them to babysit.) Taken individually, these issues are small but they have a cumulative effect on the productivity. Now when you walk #2 line, everyone is smiling except for that old grump Lonnie... he's still doing his job and figures it was high time that you finally did _yours!_ Well, Lonnie will probably never be happy, but at least you can move on to the other 486 things which need doing.

It's important that you don't take away from this chapter that you should not listen to your people. Engagement and leadership principles mandate that you must, and indeed, want to listen to them. But you will be faced with making dozens of daily decisions involving many people, and simple time constraints will prevent you from listening to each and every one about each and every concern each and every day. Some guidelines:

- Bad data will drive you to bad decisions and bad results. Your first step in making a decision must be to ensure your data is valid. *(Much more on this in Chapter 18. Spreading The Pain.)*

- If most of your operators react badly to a decision, then they might be on to something. Yep, you're capable of making a bad decision. This is also known as a mistake and you'll make 'em. How you handle these situations will set the stage for the future. Dig your heels in, ignore the obvious, and you will ensure your people keep on letting you make mistakes. Hearing your people, looking at the results as objectively as you can and acting, will keep you out of trouble.

- Don't let the fear of bad reactions hinder you from making decisions. Trying to "keep everyone happy" will lead to keeping everyone _unhappy_ because you won't be able to make _any_ decisions. This is also known as "getting wrapped up in your underwear."

- People who disagree with you are not evil – at least they are not evil _because_ they disagree with you. People may disagree for many reasons, but since most of them want to succeed, they will likely have good intentions just as you do. Don't burn them at the stake.

Succeeding chapters on improvements, managing upstream and downstream, engagement, and the danger of assumptions will show how people's diversity can benefit your operation and can actually help your personal and professional growth.

Not everybody is like you. So what? Most of them want to succeed and that makes them...just... like... you.

3

If You Don't Care, Why Should I?

There are many motivating factors that give reason to care. Responsibility, finances, security, and conscience are some of the more common ones. In this chapter we will focus on the historical adage of setting a good example. Call it the Golden Rule, ethic of reciprocity, or some other maxim of morality, but in a leadership role, we quickly accept the reality that we are judged by our peers to hold high standards. One single ingredient that can be most damaging and deteriorating at the plant level and on the plant floor, involves a sense that managers do not care. *"If you don't care, why should I?"* The formula that is needed to succeed with the plant culture requires a large dosing of *care*.

Genuine

Genuine is a word we have evolved to utilize much more in the last few years. Actually, we were taught this word by our peers over and over again as they assured us they knew the difference. It involves character and the ability to impart upon others that your intentions are whole. Not superficial, fake, laced with ulterior motives, or manipulating -which all lead to forming an aura of distrust in the plant. For the most part, none of us intend to be fake or come across as being dishonest. This is not about producing assumptions that others believe at heart your intentions are good. There should be no guess work or mystery concerning your intentions. Your actions will always speak louder than words. A typical downfall aiding in developing an atmosphere of opinion that you are not genuine – *Recall or lack thereof.*

Recall

The fast pace required on the plant floor keeps us hopping. As a manager, you are pulled in many directions and sometimes as we say – *running around like a chicken with your head cut off. (Pardon the digression for a moment as this brings to mind a good story.)*

We learned of an interesting talent that we did not know existed until an adventure building a plant in western Arkansas came about. This part of Arkansas is populated with several chicken related manufacturing plants. As we interviewed candidates to form our team, it was only natural that several in the area had worked in the chicken plants. Big Joe in particular stands out among the many. Joe was hired early on during the plant build to do odd jobs and assist in several areas including clean-up, painting, unloading trucks, and working in the kiln area. Big Joe was a good size fellow, very strong, but truly a gentle giant. He worked fast, hard, and stayed active all the time with little supervision. On one occasion, Big Joe told of his chicken catching skills from a previous job. Joe could hold 6 chickens in each hand at one time. Now that seems impossible when first heard, but as Big Joe began to explain his accomplished method of weaving the chicken's feet between each of his fingers, it became very clear that Big Joe was serious. He was not laughing or cracking a smile during any of the time he laid out the details of his unique talent. *(It was all we could do not to let loose.)* Big Joe literally ran around the plant like he was chasing chickens with their heads cut off. Quite often you might hear a supervisor say, *"Joe, Joe… slow down…you ain't chasing them blasted chickens anymore!"* Joe is a great guy and we miss him a lot. Ok, back to the beaten path of *Recall.*

How's your recall, your ability to remember important events, to summon up all the critical details of what needs to be done? Better sometime than others? You got that right and we certainly agree. *(Carl, Carl, CARL.... wake up....we're writing here!)* Maintaining good recall requires much focus and action item tracking. In Chapter 8, which deals with Engagement, we cover at length how to *improve your focus and remain task oriented.* Here we speak of focus to emphasize that struggling with recall will impact how much others sense your ability to care. Here are a few basic examples on the plant floor.

- Betty has requested that you bring her a new pair of gloves 3 times today. On her way to the time-clock, you notice that she is talking to the safety coordinator while waving a worn out pair of gloves in the air. Now your recall is *good.*

- Jim on line 3 has informed you several times today that maintenance is needed for a small problem at the unloader. After the shift ends and you are preparing your production report for the boss, you notice line 3 missed the mark considerably and the small problem added up to large downtime. Now your recall is *great.*

- You make a slight adjustment on the furnace at the beginning of the shift. You did not inform the operators or anyone else. You also forget to make a note on your action list to follow-up to see the impact of this adjustment. Later that night, after you are home, you receive a call from the plant saying that bad product is coming out of the furnace and no one knows why. Now your recall is *crystal clear. (Get your pants on, you're goin' in.)*

Taking notes, tracking changes or adjustments, following up on requests, all require *your* focus and desire to keep up. Peers will see repeated episodes of your struggle with recall as a total lack of care for them and the operation. Set the bar high for yourself to be organized and on top of your game. Recall and focus go hand in hand when *revisiting and monitoring* areas or associates that are struggling. Co-workers that do not see you offering counsel to those performing below expectations will quickly label you as weak and uncaring. Follow-up, follow-up, and you got it, follow-up.

Product Quality

Quality of your product is a large part of your voice to the customer. The customer's voice is heard loud and clear all the way up the ladder when there is an issue with quality. Want to know one of the quickest ways to let down your peers, lose respect, and win an *"I Don't Care"* t-shirt? Make repeated bad judgment calls on product that goes in the box and out to the customer. Here, another basic principle applies: *"Would you pay your hard earned money for that?"* As managers you are faced with go or no-go decisions each day. If you have hard specifications and criteria that guide you, the decision is often cut and dry. If it's a subjective call based on visual inspection and you are the final say, *be consistent.* Do not confuse other managers or operators with randomness concerning quality decisions because of your mood or how big a hurry you are in at the time. Your pride in the company, the product, the brand, and the label speaks volumes for your overall care. Holding high standards will at times cost more and generate more waste. Drive the improvements to the source of the problem and do not pass on your plant troubles to the customer. Inform your team of your care for the customer from the beginning of the process to the end. Review any quality complaints with those involved from management to production. Share the pain of customer dissatisfaction with all involved but ultimately take responsibility for the failure yourself.

Listen

- *My supervisor does not listen.*

- *The plant manager is always in his office and never comes to the plant floor to hear what we have to say.*

- *I have been saying all week that the quality on line 6 is terrible, but no one listens.*

- *The oil leaking on the floor from the press valve is going to cause an accident. I keep cleaning it up but the real problem needs to be fixed.*

If this is the buzz in your plant, not good... not good at all. Listening goes well beyond having a suggestion box and answering a few along the way. We have yet to experience more positive improvement in factories across several states and several different product lines, than those coming from the plant floor. If you underestimate your team's ability to improve the operation from within, you are not on the fast-track to victory. Yes, you will endure several conversations that involve general griping and complaining about how miserable certain individuals are and how sorry their co-workers are on the shift before them. In the midst of their needing to vent can be great solutions to historic problems as well as new ones. You may have engineered, designed, installed, or built the machine that is in production. But odds are you do not push the buttons that run it 40+ hours each week or know all the tricks that it takes to keep it running. Improvements suggested from within also have a much speedier implementation route. These improvements have staying power too as your team has a vested interest to see them succeed.

Excellence

The majority of us went into management with a complete different mindset than we came out with a few years later. At first we tend to demand excellence. We forcefully impose our authority and title upon others expecting immediate resolution to any problems. "Pick up this, pick up that, go the office, move faster, stay over, and do as I say!" And if the answer was no to any of those demands? "Why, I will just fire them all!" Sure, and the next team you get will need even more instruction, training, and leadership – which you lacked greatly. Demands attempt to invoke desired actions through fear. Commanding excellence is leadership by example. Because of your actions and demeanor, others want to naturally follow your direction. You are firm but fair. You bleed the company color but stand up for your people like they are family. Others follow your lead. Not out of fear, but out of respect and loyalty.

Remaining *genuine*, sharpening your *recall*, maintaining high *quality* standards, *listening* to your co-workers, and *commanding excellence* will be qualities that identify you constantly as someone who cares a great deal for all involved. Here are a few more examples to establish and preserve in the plant that forms an authentic culture of care.

- Cleanliness: 5S, organized areas, everything has a place, floors are shining, and equipment is well maintained. Paint and paint again as fresh color screams we have pride. Managers: pick up a broom often, empty the trash, and grab a rag to wipe down some equipment. Your hands-on approach is invaluable in showing commitment.

- Management respect hourly associates and hourly associates respect management. Everyone respects the customers, big or small. *The customers are the authorized top executives and board of directors.*

- Drive defects to the source. Do not attempt to inspect quality into the product. Take final product samples back to the sequences that created the defects and review. Keep taking samples back until the problem is resolved.

- Buy the t-shirts and caps with the company name and logo. Anyone you see wearing them outside of work, thank them. Let them know you appreciate them representing the company on and off the field.

- Be a history teacher. Know the history of the company, the founders, the owners, where it started, and how it has evolved. Teach others this history and it will show your commitment and care for the company.

- Keep your team well informed of what's happening. Monthly reports on financials, sales, production, and the overall wellness or challenges of the company help educate the team.

- And the core reason for this book, be *On The Plant Floor*. Working, training, and communicating with the troops in the field, instills more care than managing from an ivory tower.

Nobody cares how much you know, until they know how much you care.
- *Theodore Roosevelt*

4

Do The Things You Don't Like to Do

It Pays Off

Why should you do things you don't like to do? Why not shove the task off on one of those handy subordinates reporting to you? Heck, if you work hard enough avoiding a task, you can probably find someone to whitewash that fence (with apologies to Mark Twain). The answers to these questions are really pretty simple: When you avoid tasks of any kind, you will often spend more time _avoiding_ the task than the time you would spend actually _doing_ the task. And if you shove your tasks downward to subordinates, it won't take long for them to resent you. You might one day find that whitewash dumped on your car.

Tasks fall into two categories:

1. Things you must do: These can be tasks that are legal obligations such as documentation required by OSHA, Dept of Labor, and EEOC. Mandatory tasks can be those required by the company like weekly financial and production reports. Other must-dos may come from your boss. Bottom line here is you gotta do 'em if you want to avoid unemployment.
2. Things you don't have to do: These may be important to the well being of your operation, but they aren't mandatory. An example of this is Management By Walking Around (MBWA), which we heartily endorse, but you don't _have_ to do it. You might also spend daily quiet time to plan your week. Again, it is something you might do but no one requires this of you.

It will come as no surprise that most of the things you don't like to do are in Category #1, and most things you like to do are in Category #2.

Spend too much time on category #2, or cherry-pick the tasks you like out of category #1 and you will find your 40 hour week stretching into 55 hours or, more likely, your 55 hour week stretching into 70 hours. If you LIKE routinely working 70 hour weeks and don't mind when emergencies shift that work week to 100 hours, then read no further - this chapter ain't for you, Superman. (_But make sure to read Chapter 24, The Balance._)

Likewise, if you are comfortable with burdening your subordinates with tasks you yourself should be doing, then please, pass this book on to someone else as you don't belong in manufacturing. For the rest of you, please read on.

When we discuss carrying your own weight, we are not talking about avoiding delegation. No, delegation is critical in any manufacturing environment and doing it properly is a prized skill and necessary. Carrying your own weight simply means that you don't avoid doing things because you don't like them. As a manager, you will continually be rightly assigning or delegating mandatory tasks to your subordinates they will not like. You will expect those tasks to be completed. If you are unwilling to take on disagreeable tasks, then you can hardly expect your subordinates to perform their tasks to the best of their abilities.

1. Disliking job tasks usually stems from one of two reasons: Fear of failure
2. Belief that the task is "beneath" your position

Conquering the Fear of Failure

If there is one constant of the human existence, then it has to be that every single human -living and dead- has feared failure. Whether it was asking that pretty girl out for the first time or piloting an Apollo spacecraft, all of us have secretly whispered "Please, God, don't let me screw up!"

Right now you might be thinking, " I'm not about to do anything as earth-shaking as going to the moon, and a pretty girl married me long ago. All I'm trying to do is get this stupid report done!" The pretty girl you married was probably not the first one you ever asked out; you succeeded ultimately by rep-etition and the Apollo astronauts were successful, in part, because they were superbly trained. These are the keys to conquering the fear of failure - training and repetition.

Is this a new discovery? Of course not, but using them in your daily activi-ties On The Plant Floor to embrace disagreeable tasks might be something you haven't considered.

Carl-

I absolutely LOATHED preparing PowerPoint presentations. I hated the program, I hated the concept of slides, and I hated the mind-numbing banality of the presentations I attended. Hated it, hated it, hated it! Despite my feelings, the president of a company, to whom I reported, lived and died by the PowerPoint. He found it to be a powerful tool for presentations to the board of directors and investors. The president made it quite clear that my PowerPoint skills were awful and I had to improve quickly. Between my failure to satisfy his needs and the fact that I was spending up to 16 hours on Saturday and Sunday preparing bad weekly reports, I realized I needed to improve and quickly. Taking my own advice of turning to training, I signed myself up for a beginning (!) PowerPoint instructional class. The results were dramatic. My boss was happy (well, happier) and the 16 hours dropped to 2 hours that I was able to fit in on a Saturday morning. The second part of conquering my fear of failure was found in repetition. I had to do these doggone reports weekly, after all. So while I still loathe PowerPoint, I no longer fear using it. And since I am no longer afraid of producing crappy work, I don't avoid the task.

Perform a good accounting of the things you don't like to do (but must do), and think of how you can use training and/or repetition to overcome your fear. Some examples:

- Preparing weekly charts and graphs. If you need training in the program used to prepare the data, then get it! Buy a training book, get a class under your belt, ask a proficient colleague to help....but bite the bullet and get trained.

  ○ Set aside a time each week to do it. We find a Saturday morning at the plant an ideal time to catch up on paperwork. In any case, hard-schedule your time.

  ○ Make sure you have all the data you need and organize it to your liking. Nothing extends task time like running information down from multiple sources.

- Daily packed stock audits. I can't think of too many things more boring than counting your daily production. Yet it is a necessary task in many operations.

  ○ Do it the same time each and every day. And then repeat.

  ○ Carefully consider what could shorten the task. Is it better forms, access, equipment? Redesign the process to shorten it - we can almost guarantee you it is possible.

- Regular safety tours and environmental surveys. These are important for both employee safety and to avoid sanctions by insurance companies and regulatory bodies - so you gotta do 'em.

  ○ Adopt the mindset that what you are doing is important. Doing what you consider to be a waste of time will guarantee you do it poorly and rarely.

  ○ Consider an incentive plan to recognize the most improved plant sequence. Friendly competition improves results and can lessen your burden.

  ○ A safety tour should include a map and checklist. With your team, look at these tools and be critical. You may well find a quicker and more efficient route and you may find the checklist is out of date, leading you to look for things that don't exist!

Meetings

Almost everyone professes to hate meetings. What they really hate are <u>bad</u> meetings. Thousands of trees have been destroyed in producing the books that will show you how to have good meetings. We will give you just a few short tips to make meetings more palatable.

- Always, always, always have an agenda. If you can't be troubled to produce an agenda, then you shouldn't have a meeting.

- Restrict meeting time to one hour, max. Attention spans are short and most of us suffer from CRS.

- Don't allow people to interrupt one another in a meeting. Insist that people be treated with enough respect to complete their sentences. Group sessions that allow unlimited interruption have their place, but they are often called brainstorming. Brainstorming sessions are not meetings. Gripe sessions are not meetings. Laundry airing sessions are not meetings. Meetings have agendas and they last no longer than an hour.

- Have as few as possible and make them mean something. Don't schedule fact-finding meetings if you can find those facts directly with just a little effort.

So we have looked at simple techniques that can help you overcome the fear of failure and help you find ways to shorten these tasks. But what about helping others? As a manager your job is to help your people do their jobs in the most efficient way practical. Your people's job is to help their people do their jobs efficiently.

How many of you have a subordinate supervisor who spends many hours a day with tools adjusting or fixing machines? You might think he's a good guy, knows his machines, and really cares about getting those machines to run. All in all he is a great supervisor. Maybe. Or maybe not.

We had a very good supervisor we will call Mike. Mike had been at the plant for over twenty years and had been the supervisor in the packing sequence for more than eight years. He could tell you about his machines better than anyone in the plant and was at work every day with his tools, listening to his operators, helping them out, adjusting here - tinkering there. Everyone could tell you that Mike had his hand on the pulse of the department and kept things running. The problem was the department's efficiency was stagnant and well below the capacity of the equipment. When this was pointed out to Mike, he defensively responded that the machinery was old and he was doing his best. He *was* doing his best but was failing.

After much discussion we decided that some root cause failure analysis was needed. Bryan's familiarity with the plant made him the likely candidate to lead this effort, and he volunteered for the task.

Among the notable issues was the indisputable fact that some operators could run some lines better than other lines. Since operators will naturally prefer to work on lines that run "better" for them, the official plant designations of line #1, #2, #3, and #4 had degraded to Sissy's line, James' line, Bob's line, and Willie's line. Many of you will recognize an all too common situation. Over the years, through countless, maintenance interventions, and uneven wear, the 4 lines barely resembled each other even though they were designed and installed at the same time.

The effect of machinery condition had led Mike, to become a mechanic trying to keep everything running as well as possible. And he was good at it as long as he had the tools needed that day and none of his people were absent. Unfortunately, Mike didn't have many of these days. Quite often he started his shift by assigning specific people to specific lines and hoping he had enough people to run all of them. We pretty much had a nightmare situation.

We will cover the actual improvements made to the packing sequence (quite successful) in Chapter 18 where we detail entitlements, improvements and spreading the pain. For our purposes here, it suffices to say that before we began the process, Mike was at the end of his rope, discouraged and ready to leave as he believed the machines were running as well as possible. He believed we were unreasonable in expecting improvements if we were unwilling to buy new machines.

Now, Mike didn't enthusiastically accept our process, but as more and more small improvements took hold, he began to see the light at the end of the tunnel. As Bryan timed this belt speed and measured that sprocket diameter we could literally see the change taking hold in Mike. Before long, he was challenging us when we deemed an improvement finished, and soon Mike was leading the entire process.

Mike ultimately became the plant's greatest, process improvement champion, helping other supervisors with their sequences and embracing advanced six sigma training. In later conversations with Mike, a very proud man, he admitted that the reason he never initiated formal process improvement was a very simple one: he didn't know how and he was afraid that he would screw it up.

There it was - the fear of failure presenting him with a huge task he didn't like to do.

Help your people do the things they don't like to do. Invest the time and effort to educate them, insist they become part of the improvement process, and then let them run it. You will find no better satisfaction in your plant work life as that found in helping other conquer their fear.

We have said that the second reason people don't like to do certain tasks is that they consider some tasks to be beneath their position. Let us be brief and clear - if you believe something is beneath your position, resign that position immediately. You don't belong in a manufacturing plant. Manufacturing professionals understand that if a plant has a floor sweeping job, then that job is important. And if a job is important, then it is a job nobody is "too good" to do. We don't recommend that plant managers make a habit of sweeping floors, partly because they aren't very good at it, but we wouldn't give you a nickel for a plant manager that won't pick up a broom. After all, that broom handle fits a plant manager's hand just as well as it does a janitor's.

Does it fit yours?

5

You Manage Things But You Lead People

Don't Promote Failure

"You cannot manage men into battle. You manage things; you lead people."
- Grace Hopper (retired Admiral, U.S. Navy)

Far be it from us to be "politically correct" On The Plant Floor, but we believe there is a huge difference between management and leadership. We are pretty persnickety about how the two terms are used. People are not things. They live, they breathe and they think. People can lead or follow, but they can't be managed like a process. The arena of leadership may be as small as a two person assembly team or as large as the United States Army, but no supervisor or five-star general ever "managed" people - they reached the goal by leading the people who engaged in the process.

Consider a famous quote:

Lead me, follow me, or get out of my way. - General George S. Patton, Jr.

Now let's re-write it, confusing leadership with management:

Manage me, be managed by me, or get out of the way. Doesn't quite have the same ring, does it? You have the title of plant *manager* or plant *supervisor* rather than plant leader or sequence leader; and there is nothing wrong with that since you really do manage processes (things), but you achieve goals by leading people who work in the process. This is not a "touchy-feely" concept that argues a semantic difference between management and leadership. The difference is very real and a manager will not be successful without being a leader.

"There is a profound difference between management and leadership, and both are important. To manage means to bring about, to accomplish, to have charge of or responsibility for, to conduct. Leading is influencing, guiding in a direction, course, action, opinion. The distinction is crucial"—Warren Benning

Leaders and Followers

Wherever you are in the chain of command, whether a first line supervisor or a vice-president, you have a boss. Even the owner of a private company answers to someone: the customer. So by definition, all management personnel are both leaders and followers, and how well you perform as one is partially determined by how well you perform as the other. A plant manager who is not in tune with his upper management, who follows his own path without regard to corporate goals will fail as a leader – quite likely because he will be fired! But before that traumatic event (finally!), his followers in the plant will reject him because they will see his actions as not being in their best interest. He has failed both as a leader and a follower. A supervisor who excessively caters to his people's wants, ignoring transgressions or missed targets, will fail as a follower and a leader. It's likely that his group will fail to meet production goals and he will let down his boss....and at the same time, his own followers will lose respect for a weak leader they can twist around their little fingers.

Does this mean that a leader must slavishly follow their boss's every whim and desire? Certainly not! A big reason for your being placed in a leadership role is because you have been recognized to have the initiative and ability to translate plans into results, and you can't do that without a significant sense of autonomy and control. No, you cannot be a "yes man" and be an effective leader, but you must understand that you and your followers are part of a larger enterprise that depends on your group to do its part. Remember that your boss is also a follower and faces many of the same challenges as you.

"Followers who tell the truth and leaders who listen to it are an unbeatable combination."-Warren Bennis

Leading

If you Google "leadership" you will get about 139,000,000 hits. That's one hundred thirty-nine *million!* It's pretty obvious that a lot of people have ideas about leadership. And, you guessed it, we have a few ourselves. In chapter 2, Not Everybody is Like You, you saw that the people you lead and follow are individuals. But all of them have a story to tell. This is the human story of what makes them who they are and what they believe. Knowing these stories can be enormously helpful to you in making a connection. If the sweetest sound a person can hear is his own name, then surely the most gratifying thing for a follower to know is that his leader understands who he is. A true leader adds value to people by training them, challenging them to achieve, and honestly evaluating their roles in the company. Knowing their stories and finding out who they are will help you to add value. Don't expect that you will learn your people's stories by interviewing them! Walking up to someone on the floor, whipping out your notebook, and saying, "OK, Bill, I want to know all about you, so shoot!" will only ensure that you are labeled as a nut before the end of the shift. Getting to know people in a workplace isn't all that much different from getting to know them anywhere else. It takes time, effort and patience. Not everyone will open up at the same time and to the same degree (there is that pesky individuality thing again), but even the most hardened member of your team will tell his story eventually. In order to learn their stories, remember that you must be open to being teachable or all this effort will go to waste.

Evaluating people's skills and temperament and determining their role in the organization will occupy much of your time as a manager. Your company expects you to perform an annual evaluation of your people which will become a part of their permanent record. Imagine the difficulty (if you haven't already gone through it) in being accurate without knowing who they are! You do a disservice to your boss, you, and most importantly your people if you complete evaluations with incomplete knowledge. Consider being passed over for a promotion by your faceless boss because he assumed you were happy exactly where you were! This is just the sort of thing you risk doing to your people if you remain unknown to them and they to you.

The converse is true as well. Warm, fuzzy feelings are a great thing at the annual office Christmas party, but there are those unfortunate times that you need to lead somebody out the door – a termination. Knowing their story will be important here as well just in case they can be saved.

The Good, the Bad, and the Ugly

You know that you manage things and lead people, and you know their stories which have aided you to make proper evaluations. Promotions can be very good events, but they can turn bad and ugly quickly if you make a poor choice. Certainly, skills and performance will play a large choice in your decision to promote. You won't likely promote someone who is a perennially mediocre performer, but you might promote a trusted employee who has succeeded at everything he was assigned. If you don't know your people, you might promote that trusted employee right into a position for which he is wholly unsuited. Maybe he can't handle making quick decisions and spends all his time wrapped up in his underwear. Maybe he runs away from the inevitable confrontations that occur in stressful situations. Maybe he is having trouble balancing his work life and personal life in his new, more demanding roll. So he's failed….and so have you. Although there is no guarantee that any promotion will be good, you owe it to both your candidate and yourself to know if his story will likely lead him to success or disaster. These can be hard decisions, especially if a candidate has done well for you and wants to advance. But should you make a bad decision, he will suffer far more from the promotion than he will from the disappointment of being denied the opportunity. The experienced manager understands this and will often use his instinct in these situations. This instinct, or gut feeling, if you will, is probably the result of learning from their own failure. Odds are he promoted someone who failed miserably and it still haunts him. Maybe he even lost a friend over it. We will caution that gut instinct needs to be reinforced with objectivity or that feeling rumbling in your gut may just be a fart.

In those 139,000,000 Google hits, there are plenty that list leadership characteristics. Some will list 5, some will list 7, and others will list many more. There are only two, in our humble opinion, that are required for effective leaders. They are trust and integrity. Both your followers and leaders must believe they can _trust_ you to have the _integrity_ to do the right thing, no matter how hard it may be. If you don't have those two qualities then even Ronald Reagan's charisma won't be enough.

"As a leader...your principal job is to create an operating environment where others can do great things." -Richard Teerlink

This will require building that trust and integrity within the enterprise. It starts at the factory with the plant manager. Create mutual respect among team members that *commands* the management team to operate in a manner that embraces honesty. Honesty builds trust, trust builds integrity, and integrity builds character. These are qualities that no one can give or take away from you. Your choices are your own. This will require that you offer your very best. Here is a quick reference guide to major differences in being leaders and managers. Remember that you are both and the trick is in the timing.

Manager	Leader
Processes	People
Facts	Feelings
Standarization	Innovation
Position Power	Persuasion Power
Reactive	Proactive
Doing things right	Doing the right things
Rules	Values
Goals	Vision
Light a fire under people	Stoke the fire in people
Enforces Culture	Defines Cultures

"I do the very best I know how — the very best I can; and I mean to keep on doing so until the end."- Abraham Lincoln

6

Dealing With Difficult People

Need a manual for this one? We all wish there was a definitive guide to *Dealing With Difficult People,* but the truth is we live and learn in this area as much as any. And frankly, we (yeah, you too) can also be very difficult at times. This chapter will not only focus on situations with difficult people that we encounter, but will also focus on how *we* can better improve our own reactions to certain difficult situations. Did you ever walk up to a fire (problem) in the plant with a can of water in one hand and a can of gas in the other? Why do we sometimes choose the gas over the water?

With 6.4 billion people out there, conflict is a fact of life. Our emotions drive us to react with the survival instincts of fight or flight. It is our natural reaction to lash out or run away, and it takes much self-control to abate these initial feelings at the onset of conflict. Often times, higher degrees of difficulty are associated with more complex personalities. Unfortunately, complex personalities many times are connected with those of greater talent and higher intelligence. It may not be a direct reflection of intellect, but typically the smarter a person is, the more argumentative that person will tend to be. Granted, this is not always the case as well noted by a famous philosopher. (*Stupid is as stupid does. – Forrest Gump)* Regardless of your IQ, there are times when all of us are more difficult than others, and here we will attempt to learn from those occasions. Attempt to appreciate the topics covered and examples given; at times you could be on the giving end, and at others, on the receiving.

It's All About Me

Keep in mind that the majority of the time when you are on the receiving end of conflict, it's not about you. If you take difficult situations and people to heart as a personal flaw of your own, it can eat you alive. Realize that it's all about them. For whatever reason, they are displeased and choose to be negative. Their current, irritable, inner state could be something totally unrelated to events at the plant, but your luck of the draw was to be in the wrong place at the wrong time. Consider it to be random and move on. If their frustration is directed at equipment… go ahead and agree with them for the moment. The equipment obviously has no feelings and won't take it personally as opposed to returning anger back to them. Keep in the mind the amount of energy expended on a heated argument. This energy is much better served in other areas of the plant. To help manage conflict, empathize to understand the situation as seen by the key actors involved.

Ego

In a former company where we both worked, there were 3 Vice Presidents that we still consider great people, mentors, and friends. They were known to be rather difficult at times and very demanding. Since they were in VP positions, their subordinates knew to accept this and concur with their wishes. However, put all 3 of them together debating the same issue and the testosterone would be flying like crazy. They all had huge egos and when challenged, look out. Ego makes us want to respond immediately and impulsively. If conflict takes place and others are around, ego kicks into overdrive. It is critical to appreciate that, at times, it does not matter if you are right. Ask yourself, "What do I gain from being right?" Many times the answer will be nothing. "What does the other person gain if they are right?" Again, many times nothing. It is important to realize (and admit) egos grow much larger after victories in life such as success, position, political power, and money. Humbling experiences in the opposite direction of those victories tend to take care of large egos rather quickly. In Ken Blanchard's book, *"Everyone's A Coach,"* ego is defined as "Edging God out." It means whatever we do, our opinions, our thought process, our approach is only right and must be accepted, a role which God is only perfect to handle. Compassion and humility are needed to control our egos and we will speak more on this in *Chapter 23, Staying Humble.*

Time To Vent (Listen First – Speak Later)

Is it so true that once we get something off our chest that we feel better? Yes and no. If the person on the receiving end of your venting nods their head in agreement or remains quiet, yes. If the receiver stops you frequently and disagrees repeatedly, no. Let's keep it real, some folks don't know when to shut up. By now, you know those folks all too well in the plant. While we would like to remove all the negative people from the operation, we realize a lot of the plant would be shut down if this happened. Taking the approach of listening first does not mean you are always passive. In fact, remain assertive and do not tolerate rudeness or unprofessionalism. Nevertheless, there are times when someone simply wants to let off steam, so let them. Listening is a skill that requires fine tuning each day (ask your spouse). Two objectives come from hearing instead of speaking -*to connect and to learn.* Connecting with someone will go a long way toward problem solving. Try to relate to their concerns by letting more of the conflict reveal itself through listening. This is not an attempt to get inside someone's head and analyze how big a whack job you think they may be. Don't just listen for the facts, listen to the person. It simply allows them to vent and eventually they will get to the root cause. Each conversation or episode of conflict you engage in with a difficult person is a learning experience. Often times, learning does not come with experience, but in the case of dealing with difficult people, it tends to make a lasting impression. Are you a good listener? Here are a few tips.

- Remove distractions: turn off the phone(s), close the laptop, and pay attention.

- Put aside prejudices: do this as far as possible in that you may generally not like the person, so focus on their words instead of who's saying them.

- Remain a student: be willing to continually learn from others: John Wooden said it very well. *"It's what you learn after you know it all that really counts."* There is a chance that this person is conveying dissatisfaction that others have also been feeling but have kept contained.

- Undervalue talking / don't interrupt: Abraham Lincoln is considered one of the greatest leaders of all time and offered this advice: *"When I am getting ready to reason with a man, I spend one third of my time thinking about what I will say and two thirds thinking about what he is going to say.* (Good advice indeed, listen twice as much as you speak.)

- Suspend judgment: do not find the solution 30 seconds into the conversation.

- Ask questions at the end: review briefly the points made by the speaker and ask questions on possible solutions or give possible reasons for their disappointment.

Intellectual Patience vs. Emotional Patience

Difficult people come from all directions, above and below our levels. Most of us mentally accept the need to have patience when dealing with difficult people. The deterrence to having patience is often emotionally driven. Certain words fuel the fire and emotions begin to flame. More often than not, difficult people who report to you know most of these words. Meaning they already know what gets your blood boiling and may immediately test your patience. Expect this and prepare for it by assertively starting the conversation with certain ground rules. Call the meeting and set the agenda to include:
1. Main purpose: why we are here - you plan to stay on topic.
2. Do not rush the discussion but set a time limit.

3. Explain that the conversation must remain calm and without personal insult or you will end the meeting.

4. Remind them in a non-threatening way that you are still the boss. Refer to your duties instead of your position. For example, explain that reconciling this problem is in the best interest of the plant as well as your responsibility.

5. Now sit back and listen with patience.

Setting the agenda for the discussion with a subordinate does not mean you are attempting to manipulate or monopolize the conversation. It establishes your concern for an issue and the need to hear their voice in an effort to resolve. Using these 5 tips will help control your emotions so that they do not override your intellect.

The Difficult Boss

Could be yours, or could be you. Subordinates are not the only source of difficulty. First, let's look at difficult bosses. What makes them difficult? Basically it boils down to their *level of unpredictable involvement*. At times they are seemingly micro-managing to the point of making every move for you. In the other extreme, they are not accessible when you need a decision before moving forward. And worse yet, mixed signals are sent by reacting inconsistently to similar circumstances so that you do not know what to expect. How many times have you wondered how they got to their position? Several, but how many times have your subordinates wondered the same about you? Probably just as much, so dealing with difficult bosses is a reality we all face in our careers at one time or another. How can we manage these frustrations and thrive?

- Hide? As much as you may want to keep your head down and under the radar, avoidance may not work. Several times over the years we have had bosses that we felt surely would be replaced at any time. Most of them outlasted us, so avoid crawling into the basement to ride out the storm. Accept that you may have to manage the manager, and being a difficult person is part of their personality.

- Approach issues as a *discussion and not a confrontation*. When you are criticized, do not let emotions cause confrontational reactions. Criticism of your work must mean they have a different belief in the methods for how the work should be done. While you might not agree, or in fact, their methods may not be solutions; it is still their own idea and you should accept it as discussion instead of confrontation.

- *Walk The Company Line.* When challenged about decisions, constantly refer to the best interest of the enterprise as your intent. Attempt to think and manage on a level that your boss or their boss does. Bleed the company colors and it will continue to show through. Walking the company line will put all personal agendas aside regardless of the title.

- *Agreement vs. Decision*: try to reach an agreed goal for a path forward. This does not mean a final decision is firm and written in stone. It's sometimes a compromise from two strong arguments of how to resolve problems or make improvements. Often, more than not, a mixed implementation of their ideas and your own come forward.

- *Self-evaluation vs. Facts*: are you meeting the performance goals? Examine your own performance against the boss's disparagement and ask yourself, "Am I getting the job done?" Without going into details or giving the background, ask co-workers their view of your performance. Regardless of our positions, accomplishments, talents, or titles, we all need a check-up.

- *Document Everything*: if you consider your boss to be difficult in more ways than one, you may also lack trust. Document your discussions in detail as unfortunately they may be needed at some point.

- *Containment*: do not bare your soul to others concerning problems with your boss. This will no doubt work its way up the food chain and a difficult situation will soon grow to become impossible. This takes extraordinary reserve but is in the best interest of the plant. Others will lose confidence in your ability to execute knowing you are resisted upstream.

Union Negotiations

Undoubtedly some of the most difficult people that we have dealt with came during union contract renewals. If you merge with or are purchased by another company that operates non-union plants, all of a sudden you are the ugly duckling and in the spotlight. Your VP wants to know why you have to negotiate. "Just tell em' to go strike if they don't like it and we'll replace the whole bunch!" While this might be tempting, it is often a no-win situation (and quite possibly illegal) and creates a plant impossible to manage. On one occasion of contract talks, the VP of Manufacturing insisted on being at our local negotiations. We pushed back letting him know that if he was sitting at the table during negotiations, the union would expect an immediate answer. If he stayed at the corporate post, we could buy time that allowed us to determine better alternatives. Fortunately, he agreed and we worked through the contract renewal with, as always, a give and take approach.

Dealing with difficult situations and people in a union or non-union plant is inevitable. Seemingly, the company and the union can appear to come from different planets. If you believe you can form a lasting bond and trust between the two, good luck. Taking the approach to coexist in spite of the differences is in the best interest of the company and the union. Keep in mind that your job and the union's job are similar – protect the work environment. Both sides need to recognize difficult employees as being problematic. Discussing these issues directly with the union president or local representative is your best route to dealing with malcontents. Having the union reign in and control these difficult people is your best route to resolution. They also understand that it makes them look bad and can hurt membership.

Toxic Employees

Some employees are simply poisonous. They are active at working to deteriorate the culture of the plant. Their goal is to infuse constant chaos on the plant floor and they are good at it. Their venom is well aimed and intentional. This cannot be tolerated and after several attempts to correct the situation, you realize you must terminate the virus before it spreads any further. You have been documenting the problems each step of the way, right? Collateral damage to the rest of the team is unacceptable, make the change.

In summary, dealing with difficult people is, in fact, difficult but not impossible. There are several books, courses, and training programs on this topic but no definitive guide. Your ability to control emotions from the giving and receiving side of difficulty is a key technique for not adding gas to the fire. Accept that the issues from difficult people are selfish and not about you, so do not take it personally. Ego has to take a few steps back when dealing with difficult people. The same pride and stubbornness from ego can be what makes you difficult at times also. Allowing someone to vent about an issue is not a sign of giving in to demands. This requires great listening skills such as suspending judgment to reach resolution. While you may have intellectual patience (the knowledge that you should be patient), you may need to work on emotional patience in order to execute. This is true whether the difficult people work above or below you.

7

The Walk

The title of this chapter could be called Dealing With Conflict or Managing Your Emotions. While these titles sound all too familiar, conflict is a reality in the plant as well as in life. Tension does not only come from the other side of the fence either. Quite often we (yeah-you too) initiate the friction in an area by letting our pride, emotions, and stubbornness override the need to maintain continuity and professionalism.

Do you recall as a child sometimes just wanting to run away from home? We all did and sometimes went through with it, but more often than not, got shaky knees and raced back mighty quick. However, taking "*The Walk*" did us good and allowed us time to put events in the proper perspective and to do a reality check as well. Later in life we find that walking, hiking, or even jogging can be relaxing and refreshing. It is not an attempt to run away from our problems or to hide from confrontations. It's the change of scenery, the breath of fresh air, the time to cool off, the time to take *The Walk*.

Bryan-

In all the plants I have worked, production lines span anywhere from 100 to 400 ft in length. It takes several steps to cover a line of this nature each day on the plant floor. A typical shift involves walking up and down the lines to collaborate with all the operators and review any mechanical or quality issues at each section. Also in the plants in which I have worked, we had large furnaces (kilns) that were 200 to 300 ft in length. Between two of these kilns in Jackson, TN, was a wide and long aisle leading from one set of sequences to others. It is down this aisle that I learned The Walk.

If you are an introvert, the plant floor can be difficult. You will need to interact with an extensive variety of individuals ranging from solid, hard-working people to those who seemingly have only one objective-making your life miserable. While this may not be their sole objective, it surely appears that way to you, and in your opinion, they do a great job of it. Whether you label them a troublemaker, provoker, pain in the ...neck, etc, they remain your coworkers. This is not only speaking of hourly associates either. We all have our days: a bad argument at home, financial issues, hard drive crashed, Cowboys lost (again), and on and on. At these times we conceivably await a reason to just go off on someone.

Life at work is not much different than life away from work when we let our emotions run amuck. We find ourselves working on damage control after the dust settles and trying to regain unity. In a leadership role when we lash out, we lose on several levels. Here are a few of the most principal ones.

Confidence

What often takes years to build and gain? Confidence. Full trust and assurance are terms to keep in mind when speaking of confidence. You have great expectations for those reporting to you. Each day you compel them to perform in a safe and effective manner in order to reach the needed performance levels. You also rely upon them to be a large part of the voice to the customer with the quality of their work. This entails you to build their trust and assurance in you, the boss that leads, guides, and directs. We mentioned being an introvert earlier in the context of being on the plant floor. It will be extremely hard to build trust and assurance in others in the manufacturing environment if they rarely see you in the process. However, if they see you more often than not in a frenzy and struggling to get along with others; what confidence can they have in your ability to manage a problem, a sequence, a shift, or a plant?

Respect

In a critical chapter in which we title, "*Building The Culture*", we are, for the most part, referring to respect. Therefore, as someone in a leadership role, you should command respect. We all know too well that earning the respect of your peers takes time and much patience. Often this ends up being one step forward and two steps back when we appear constantly rattled and allow unrestrained comments to others or equipment to get out of hand. If you do not maintain respect at all levels, never underestimate your ability to see a sequence, shift, or plant take serious steps in the wrong direction.

Control

We are bought by another company and the new VP of Manufacturing arrives at the plant for the first time. As he walks into a conference room where we have assembled the management team, his first words are something like this. "Well hello team, I'm the Vice President of Manufacturing. Who runs the show here, who's in charge?" Quite an introduction, and it is clear he expects the local leadership to fully understand their accountabilities. It is an awesome responsibility to be in control of an area in a manufacturing plant and especially to be the plant manager in control of the whole "shebang." If you have been there, or are currently there, you appreciate this statement immensely. If you signed up for the gig in order to acquire more power and/or more money, by now you are sorely disappointed. It is far more about having a larger voice and more impact on the plant and the company as a whole. You can easily forfeit control of your area when anger or rage is involved. Stay in control, run your emotions so you can run your area.

Confidence, respect, control – all essential in your ability to succeed as a leader. Easy right? We are not psychologists and a long way from being experts on managing emotions. But we can, in fact, speak proficiently on the subject because of our often notable success in learning things the hard way. Early in the chapter we mentioned the long production lines and the long aisle between the kilns. TheWalk is a method we have found successful for ourselves as well as many others over the years. The aisle between the kilns became a refuge at the plant in Jackson. If there was an occasion-and there were many-that created an opportunity to show disappointment, disgust, or anger, that 200 foot walk helped clear the air considerably.

It took several stumbles, falls, and bruises to learn to walk. It is not intuitive nor the natural instinct amidst confrontation. Do not misunderstand us, as we wholeheartedly support confrontation when needed to spearhead forward momentum. But there is a place for this and preferably not on the plant floor. Show the same respect to others that you appreciate, and confront the issue in private. Mold this into the plant culture as a vital policy of mutual respect on the plant floor.

There could be many underlying reasons that we all struggle to maintain our composure and to manage anger as well as frustrations at the factory level. The reasons are different for everybody and may be a combination of various dynamics. Developing the ability to realize when these emotions are coming on is a key to learning improved reactions to difficult situations. We've all been there, but being conscious of it at the time is a different story. Your heart rate is climbing, your muscles tighten, you get red hot in the face-you are about to lose it. Now is the time to invoke the childhood lesson of biting your tongue. In other words, take "*The Walk.*" As mentioned, you are not running away from the problem but are more willing to realize your immediate response will not be part of the solution. i.e. *that's just stupid! Did you get hit in the head? Fire Bubba, he's an idiot!*

Let's look at some specific examples that can cause your blood to boil on the plant floor.

• Frequent downtime on the same piece of equipment for the same reason

• Lack of talent on your shift – operators and maintenance

• Mistakes (operational, quality, safety, waste, etc...)

• Difficult personnel – slow, argumentative, sloppy

• No shows = double whammy as you now have to ask the difficult personnel to work OT

Any of these ring a bell? You betcha, and one or all give plenty of reason just to go off on someone. Let's consider instead to implement *The Walk* into a real-time scenario at the plant.

ON THE PLANT FLOOR

Two co-workers, Bubba and Earl, are working on line 2 in the assembly sequence. This sequence recently instituted a bonus system based on piece rate, allowing operators to earn more pay per hour for increased production. (BTW, a bonus or piece rate system can create multiple failures if not planned well and managed closely. We are not in favor of these.) Bubba follows Earl in the assembly sequence; thus, if Earl falls behind in his area, it impacts Bubba's output and paycheck. Earl is struggling quite a bit one night to keep up, and about midway through the shift, Bubba is pretty much ready to stomp Earl. Fortunately, you, the line supervisor, are on the plant floor a great deal and recognize production is down. You also recognize that Bubba is pissed now that the bonus rate is in place. It is common knowledge that Earl is very dependable, gets along well with others, but is slower than some of his co-workers. Bubba only sees his paycheck down by two 12 packs. Don't get us wrong, we are not defending Earl for being slow or reprimanding Bubba for wanting high productivity rates. It's a real life example we all have faced in a balanced, work team containing various strengths and weaknesses. On this occasion, *The Walk* comes in handy just as Bubba starts singing "Earl Had To Die" and just before Earl pees his pants. You step into the fire zone. "Bubba, Bubba, I said Bubba! Hold your horses and let's take a walk." You place a utility operator on the line to fill in for Bubba as you begin the walk. Just as Bubba begins to unload on you about how sorry and dumb Earl is, you inform Bubba of the following. "Bubba, you and I are taking a walk to the back of the plant. It will take about 5 minutes to get there, and during this walk we will not say a word to each other or anyone else. My hope, which is in your best interest, would be by the time we reach the back of the plant, you have cooled off. You have realized Earl is doing the best he can with the equipment in his section." Sure enough, you reach the back of the plant and Bubba is still pissed, but not nearly as much as he was on the line. You now allow Bubba to vent for a moment, and then put the occurrence into perspective. "Bubba, you know we rotate all the operators on the assembly line, and the section Earl is in now is one of the more difficult. Earl may not be as fast as you and some of the other operators, but who comes over to help you in your section each time you get behind? Who fills in for you if you need to go to the restroom outside of break times? This (I might add) is becoming too frequent lately." Of course, Bubba rattles on some more about what all he does for the company and how his sincere intention is to get the most production for the plant. While this is perhaps true, Bubba's hard to get along with for you and for others. You just did Bubba, Earl, yourself, and several other co-workers a world of good by taking Bubba for a walk.

As managers and supervisors, we deal with these type problems multiple times per day. More so, we face challenges in controlling our emotions as we attempt to meet the expectations from several different levels. Supervisors following each other in the same sequence often feel they are getting a raw deal. Why were all the changeovers left for my shift? Why is the place in such a mess without clean-up efforts? Why is the line not supplied with enough materials to run for awhile? Dissatisfaction among supervisors at the same level is all too common. Any confrontation between supervisors on the plant floor will allow subordinates to play off of this and stir the pot even more. This must be highly discouraged, and should again, become a part of the plant culture to avoid.

Another difficult but common front line supervisor example is to keep your emotions in check in front of your boss. Learning to show and relay passion instead of discontentment is a skill to fine tune often. A specific time to do this is during conversations with your boss. Make sure to mention your passion and simply state that your that intentions are pure. Don't assume this is a given and well known. If your boss often sees you in a panic in your area, it's not encouraging at all. However, a good thing to keep in mind is some advice we learned several years ago: walk fast and look nervous. We could say keep a rag in your pocket too, as these old school methods still show, or at least suggest, strong active engagement. Depending on what type of boss you have, you may find the need to utilize *The Walk* quite often. Especially if you are on one of those late in the evening cell phone calls regarding today's performance—or lack of performance. Remaining professional, not taking business as personal insults, and conveying passion instead of frustration, are all much easier when taking a few deep breaths during *The Walk*. However, if you are in a meeting that your boss is leading, and he decides to send a few, strong comments in your direction; this is not the time to invoke the walk. Now, after the meeting would be a perfect time for a long one -maybe a couple.

Let's summarize the use of *The Walk* for multiple purposes. It is not just a good tool for operators such as Bubba. In fact, it is more often a good tool for managers. In addition, all the frustrations mentioned earlier such as equipment problems, operational mistakes, quality issues, and difficult personnel-including other managers below and above your level—are reason enough to let your emotions get out of hand. When this happens, we risk losing groundwork in areas that took considerable time to build. *Confidence, respect,* and *control* are fundamental connections to your success as a leader. We claim no mastery of emotions on our side and wholly concede through experiences of our own that managing these is much easier said than done. Nonetheless, cultivating present moment awareness of what's going on inside of you at the onset of the incident should allow you to react more productively. Take *The Walk,* for yourself and for others.

Engagement

Daily Involvement With The Troops In The Field

There are many definitions for the term *engagement,* but the one that best serves here is *the act of involvement and commitment.* Here are some behavioral steps to help us and our coworkers support daily *engagement:*

- Attention to details – walk the sequences often

- Commit to commanding excellence – yes Commanding not Demanding

- Stay involved with special projects – not just the ones you are leading

- Demonstrate personal and professional improvement –done learning? you are done

- Initiate problem solving and/or conflict resolution – not just problem finding

- Listen to the process owners and operators – really listen and hear

- If meetings are required, when possible, have them on the floor – keep them short

- Be a student of the process – know your equipment, the output rates, downtime issues, operator training needs, and quality resolutions.

Actively remaining *engaged* will require a considerable amount of time on the plant floor. This will reduce the number of meetings, conference calls, and time in the office sitting on your blessed assurance. A common routine might involve getting to work early before 6:00 am and making sure to walk the floor and visit with the third shirt production teams. From a plant manager's position, it is important to locate the sequence supervisor first and touch base with them. Going directly to the operators or maintenance staff first can often cause tension with the supervisor whom is ultimately most responsible for their area. If you cannot find the supervisor in the area, after some time, this is a problem that should be addressed immediately. As the plant manager, you are constantly working to create an atmosphere and expectation that the front supervisor's position is active with their personnel, equipment, and quality. After getting a summary of the third shift indicators from the supervisor, such as safety, quality, production output, and maintenance issues, make sure to spend time speaking to the operators. Often as plant manager, your role can be a lot less technical and much more personal. In general, we all appreciate someone that is concerned about our well being both on and off the field. Get to know the people that more directly affect the bottom line. Be on a first name basis with those in the same plant. Everyone loves to hear their name spoken, especially by the plant manager. Of course, ask about their families and try to find some common interest that you can share. Do not be the one everyone dreads to see walking into their areas. Also spend time asking them about their shift, the equipment, the quality, and their thoughts for continuous improvement. If you consider your actions to be best kept at a distance and not getting to close to the team, consider again. Care is expected from both sides.   *What keeps us on the plant floor and off the plant floor?*

ON	OFF
Equipment	Meetings
Operators	Conference Calls
Quality	Reports
Production	Email
Comfort	Comfort
Habit	Habit

Notice that *Comfort* and *Habit* are listed in both categories. In manufacturing, your comfort level of being on the plant floor has to be high. Over the years, we have seen managers and supervisors that appear out of place on the plant floor but right at home in their office or meetings. Typically these managers / supervisors were weaker in the areas that we will refer to as the critical **PRO**s.

- People

- p**R**ocess

- pr**O**duct

It is very difficult to be fully engaged in something which makes you uncomfortable. Whether it is a lack of training, a lack of knowledge, or unfortunately, a lack of interest, it once again falls on leadership to do the things you may not want to do. Set the expectation that being a **PRO** at the plant is a requirement, not an option. Managers that find a high comfort level on the floor add maximum value to constant process improvements.

Habit refers to a daily routine. It's true that bad habits are awfully hard to break, but instilling good habits is no walk in the park. Here we will mention an example of the great 5S methodology that most of you have been exposed to or trained in.

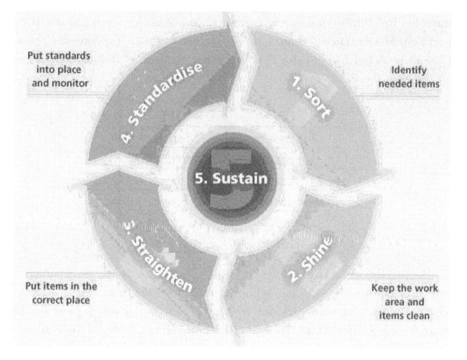

5S is one of the best examples of forming very good habits within a manufacturing plant. It develops principles of organization, pride, and commitment. It will require constant engagement to sustain this program.

Bad habits can be referred to as = CONs.

• Conflict

• cOnfusion

• coNtention

Tolerating an environment that has incessant conflict, persistent confusion, and that thrives on contention will spread a wildfire of bad habits within the operation. We all are creatures of habit, and luckily, studies show that forming good habits typically only takes 3 weeks.(1) Develop of a list of good habits you would like to initiate in your area. Champion these habits for the first 3 weeks, and then consider rotating leaders to sustain the movement so that it becomes a part of the culture. Good habits require *full engagement* to the level that we are physically energized, mentally focused, and emotionally connected with the heartbeat of the plant.

Are we putting forth the effort to make rounds on the floor each day? Visiting the various sequences of the process, hearing the voice of the operators, and reviewing the status of the equipment? Paying attention to the overall organization of the sequence will require daily engagement with purpose. Purpose creates destination. Everyone wants to know where they are headed. Earlier we mentioned events that can keep us off the plant floor. Meetings, conference calls, reports, and emails are just a few examples. All of these are required at times and should be expected in the plant. However, they can be limited or set at times less disruptive to the action on the plant floor. Email traffic alone can consume an enormous amount of time and energy. Are the majority of your emails required? Could a quick phone call (or walk to the plant floor if it's internal) resolve in 5 minutes what might take considerably more time by email? In chapter 12, "Emails Are Evil," we will dive deeper into this subject offering escape routes from this dreary maze of clicking send and receive.

Asking too much (Demand Exceeds Capacity)?

How can I possibly get all of this done each day? Do you have an idea how many different directions I am pulled? I am busting my tail to keep up! This place would fall apart without me! Ok...ok...ok.... we hear you loud and clear and have worn the same T-shirt. Let's talk about ways to improve focus and reduce waste. Waste in the areas of time, energy, and job scope are costing you.

<u>Time / Energy / Job Scope</u> = *Operators, Fire Fighting, Turning Wrenches*

You're wasting time. No doubt, we all do it and many opportunities are missed that could create positive results. There are volumes of works on Time Management and several offer great techniques for improvement. Here we continue to focus on the plant floor and events that cost us valuable time.

Operators

Some operators require *much* more attention than others. Either they need constant supervision to ensure they are producing at a high level, they desire your constant approval, or they can't get along with others. You should be accessible to your associates and facilitate the needed decisions expected. However, if you find yourself spending time over and over again with the same employee for the same problem, take a hard stance. Assure them of your desire to see them succeed but let them know that you will not waste valuable, personal and company time on repeated occurrences. Don't get caught spending 80% of your energy with 20% of your workforce.

Fire Fighting

Einstein's definition of insanity is doing the same thing over and over and expecting different results. Do you fight the same fires over and over each day that consume valuable time and energy? Of course, and we are sure you are busting your can to work through them. Do you have the resources at your disposal to properly extinguish the fire? Material problems, equipment problems, supplier problems, engineering problems, etc...? They all point the finger in one direction – at you. Getting the right players on the field is a must in order to survive in today's production world. Pride and stubbornness need to quickly take a backseat to requesting assistance from local resources inside the plant, from corporate help, engineering support, or from vendors. Fighting the fire alone will just burn the place down, perhaps slowly, but surely.

Turning Wrenches

More old school, but knowing your equipment to the point of being able to work on it safely and efficiently strengthens expertise in the operation. Managers and supervisors should be fully engaged in the installation, performance, and maintenance of their equipment. Success lies in being very hands-on and equipped to provide the troubleshooting and training needed for others. This will also serve you well if expansion or equipment upgrades are needed since you will have great knowledge and voice in the decision making. HOWEVER, being your own mechanic day in and day out will cost you and the company valuable time needed managing the process or plant as a whole. Spending 4 hours each day working on mill #3 pulls you away from the other equipment and operators that are potentially failing. We all gravitate to what we are most comfortable doing. Some managers only feel they are doing their job if they are turning wretches, and frankly, do a great job pulling maintenance. Quite often the sequence stations and supervisors do not have the expertise or tools to safely or adequately work on their equipment. How many times have you turned a small problem- that should have taken 10 minutes to resolve - into being down the whole shift? The authors have both hands raised. *(Carl has both feet in the air, also!)* Call for help. Get mechanics and electricians involved at the onset, and if not resolved timely, get the maintenance manager involved. Be hands-on, but know when it costs you and the company significant time needed in other areas. Appreciate the problems that are out of your job scope.

Focus

Now that you have a few tools on how to reduce waste, conserve energy, and recognize your job scope limitations, let's move forward to improving every day focus. Engagement requires a constant focus on the task at hand; a determination to stay on the beaten path and to not get pulled into every wild goose chase that comes your way. This is difficult in the plant with so many moving parts and pieces to place in the puzzle. Your ability to remain focused does not solely depend on your own actions in the plant; it depends on your ability to quickly determine what you should and should not be involved in. Distractions come from all directions including co-workers, our boss, the corporate office, and much of the time, from outside of work. Let's first address those from outside of work.

In Chapter 24, *The Balance*, we cover at length our grown belief in having a life *outside* of work. This does not mean concentrating on life *outside* of work while your responsibilities at the plant take second place. Knowing when to take time off, when to leave early, when to answer outside calls, and so on, impact your ability to excel for the plant. Certain freedom comes with management compared to being an hourly employee. Specific examples during the day involve taking breaks, lunch, coming off the plant floor, and leaving the plant during work times. While it sounds old school, (we are) following a general rule of respecting the time clock works well. If your co-workers cannot schedule a doctor, dentist, a haircut, or other routine appointment during normal work hours, should you? Understanding that you may work from dusk to dawn and arranging these appointments may be quite the challenge; there are exceptions. However, coming back to work after being on vacation for a week and leaving early for a haircut??? Schedule your engagements *outside* of work time, so that you remain focused and engaged *in* the plant.

Distractions at the plant causing us to lose focus are all too common. We should have an open door policy. Pulling out your day planner or answering emails on your smart-phone when someone wants your advice for 10 minutes is arrogant. As we often say, "The whole world is busy, cry me a river." It is true you are busy, and at times, busier than others. Sometimes you do need to shut your door and hard schedule conversations with others. Be goal and task driven; work from a list. Keeping up with a basic action item and to-do list can be dynamic. Refer to the list often and adjust as needed. Do not eliminate an item that you listed unless you have completed it. We have tools today, including computers and cell phones, that allow us to program events and reminders in order to assure that we stay focused and task oriented. Adjust your time with co-workers if it constantly pulls you away from being engaged in critical areas on the plant floor. This is not to say be rude or in a state of panic all the time as this can build shields around you. The old saying, "Don't let any grass grow under your feet," is good to keep in mind. If you stay on the move, knocking out your action list and working on the plant floor, your focus remains high. Focus is a self-discipline that requires frequent refining.

In closing this chapter, let's address a sensitive area. Does the corporate office sidetrack you often? Does your boss sidetrack you often? Yes, to both? Certainly, and you will need to tread lightly here. *(Or have a backup plan – see Chapter 21 In Or Out Of The Organization.)* Engagement on the plant floor can often be reduced by numerous meetings, conference calls, and one-on-one sessions with your boss.

"I cannot do my job sitting in meetings all day."

Must we have this meeting every Monday morning during production start-up?

3 conference calls in the same day???

Anytime my boss calls and says, "I will not take much of your time because I know you are extremely busy," I know it will be a long night.

All of the above examples are dreadfully familiar in the life of those in plant management. Have you developed a relationship upstream that promotes your ability to tactfully push back? If you are relatively new in your role or have a new boss, you more than likely have not, since this will take considerable time and patience. If you are new in your role, here is a tip to better communication with your boss. Ask in what form he/she would like their communication. Email, phone call, or leave me alone? The boss will be presently surprised from your asking. You were chosen for your role for many possible reasons, not least of which is your experience and perceived ability. Be secure and genuine with the corporate office and your boss, and it will show. Make up excuses or give answers without supporting data, and you will be transparent in the wrong way.

Propose alternative times and schedules for meetings, conference calls, and conversations upstream. Here are a few tips to help you remain task and routine driven without losing grace with superiors. Request that unless it's an emergency, you would like to be fully engaged in the plant during:

- *Mondays*

- *At shift changes*

- *Equipment installations / start-up*

- *Training sessions with your staff*

- *At wrap up time in the evening (from x to x o'clock)*

In this chapter we have covered *engagement as the act of involvement and commitment.* This requires developing productive routines each day that endorse task oriented events such as those listed in the first paragraph. The critical **PRO**s of engagement are your **P**eople, p**R**ocess, and pr**O**duct. Habits that deter engagements are **CON**s – **C**onflict, c**O**nfusion, and co**N**tention. Your efforts to reduce waste in the areas of time, energy, and job scope will be constant in order to remain focused. Getting sidetracked by our co-workers, our boss, the corporate office, and personal issues outside of the plant can kill focus. Develop tactful approaches to managing your schedule wisely so that you remain at a high level of engagement on the plant floor.

(1) Dr. Maxwell Maltz – Pyscho-Cybernetics

Full Disclosure

Developing An Atmosphere Of Trust & Integrity

Full disclosure as defined in computer security means to disclose all the details of a security problem which are known. It is a philosophy of management completely opposed to the idea of *security through obscurity*. The theory behind this example involves exposing vulnerabilities openly so that quicker fixes are found and better security prevails. In real estate terms, full disclosure is the act of providing all material information about an article or property intended or proposed to be transferred, which may influence the decision of the buyer or proposed buyer. In accounting principles, full disclosure states that you should include in an entity's financial statements all information that would affect a reader's understanding of those statements. Consider these definitions and their relevance to manufacturing now. Do we recognize that problems are more evident when the plant culture endorses full disclosure compared to sweeping everything under the rug? Do we encourage our team to openly provide all the information needed about a concern or problem instead of *just handling it*? Is the environment such that critical information impacting the plant's ability to excel is withheld? Do lab test results show enough repeatability to enter the manufacturing arena?

In this chapter we hope to encourage full disclosure at the plant level in the areas of problem solving, reduction of surprises, revelations of technical findings, and te avoidance of laundry lists. Disclosure in this context is not in reference to personal details about individuals such as their salary or work history. As always, these should remain confidential.

Setting the bar high and asking hard questions is much easier *accepted as expected when the plant culture* promotes *full disclosure* without fear of reprimand. This will require building continual trust and integrity within the Institution. It starts at the factory with the plant manager.

It is the absolute duty of the plant manager to instill in each team member that accountability includes never covering-up or masking problems that impact the company or customer. Refusing to acknowledge weaknesses, putting band aids on real issues, and accepting mediocrity, unquestionably delays forward progress. The ultimate goal of full disclosure is to ensure that the team understands the need to fully address core issues impacting the bottom line and quality to the customer. It will draw a line in the sand for the all too familiar *"it's just always been like that."* It wholly supports the power of persistence.

It's not that I'm so smart; it's just that I stay with problems longer. - Albert Einstein

Here are some tools for implementing full disclosure within the plant.

1. Support openness of failures. (Do not crucify members for admitting mistakes or finding problems.)

2. Expose yourself to good thinkers. These are change agents.

3. *(I can give you a six-word formula for success: Think things through – then follow through.) - World War I Flying Ace / Eddie Rickenbacker*

4. Convey that saying "I don't know" is not a weakness. It is a dangerous place to be when you are surrounded by those that "don't know that they don't know".

5. Teach that the plant ethics include full disclosure that requires personal discipline.

6. Recruit, interview, and hire problem solvers. Their experience and skill gravitate to working on solutions. They thrive to put the complex puzzles together.

(What we do on some great occasion will probably depend on what we already are; and what we are will be the result of previous years of self-discipline. – H.P. Liddon)

Full Disclosure Is Not A Weapon

Our focus continues to be *On The Plant Floor* as the plant manager will need to discern a great deal of information from corporate as it relates to the plant. As plant manager, you well know there are many situations that should ride solely on your shoulders. Fortunately, many times discussions that might impact your operation subside; eg, "If sales do not improve this quarter, we will need to reduce the workforce." You work up a plan in preparation for the reduction, but large orders come in and the cut-back is avoided. Other examples include quality issues that might initially indicate a complete re-tooling need within the operation. However, the customer determines that the problem is manageable with minimal changes on their side compared to delayed deliveries from you. These are not times to utilize a method of full disclosure to beat your team over the head as a scare tactic. Demanding improvements on the floor from corporate drama that has not yet allowed all the facts to be unveiled, creates mixed signals of leadership. Are you as plant manager running the plant or is someone from corporate doing your job? No doubt, at times, you feel this could go either way. Discernment is the key to recognizing when disclosure from corporate strategy is needed within the plant. Unnecessary crises result in a loss of momentum and morale.

Permitting other managers and supervisors within the plant to apply disclosure to their workforce as a weapon is wrong. For example, a supervisor that is constantly making mistakes feels the need to run and tell you immediately for protection. They seem to always blame failures downstream on their operators and carry a list of those "to-be-fired" in their pocket. Explain to them your disappointment in this approach and that disclosure does not mean baring their soul every time there is a problem. Reacting to a supervisor that attempts disclosure (even the one in this example that does it poorly) by demoting them or firing them can quickly ruin the idea of full disclosure. Do not punish those that deliver bad news, or you become the boss that cannot deal with problems or the one that just doesn't want to hear it. This develops the opposite culture of full containment.

Reducing Surprises

Another substantial benefit from applying full disclosure is the prevention of invariable surprises. Nothing makes a plant manager's or supervisor's day go south more than hearing something such as, "I thought the noise from the motor was minor and would go away." This is after a large motor fails completely, and of course, you do not have one on the shelf. Keeping team members engaged in the plant at a level that encourages constant communication, detailed focus, and discovery of problems goes a long way toward reducing surprises. This especially applies to safety and quality as it endorses the detection of potential failures. Quite often disclosure is withheld because of the fear of more work. "If I tell the boss about these problems, he will hold me accountable for helping to fix them and it will take forever."

Problems are only opportunities in work clothes.

— Henry J. Kaiser

Technical Disclosure

Many talented and technical people struggle with divulging information that could be critical to success. They continue to lean on the old adage that "information is power." Somehow they feel vulnerable if they train others to be experts in the process too. Our experience has been, more times than not, bad test results give more information than most positive test results. Regrettably, if the testers are in charge or tasked with resolving a problem, they feel threatened by failed test results they initiated and performed.

Let's consider that research and development is working under a tight and demanding timeline to introduce a new product or process into production. Isn't it amazing how absolute requirements become less so when the deadline is near? Do you think knowing that only 50% of the trials or formulas in the lab were repeatable is critical to the plant? Of course, but have you ever been on the receiving end of not being privy to experimental test results before they come to the plant? Like us, you probably have been more times than you prefer and fully understand the magnitude of the cost consequences.

It requires strong upper leadership to command a productive relation-ship between R&D and manufacturing. Having worked on both sides, we can say that a team well-balanced in both areas has the best chance for success. Infusing within R&D, members such as transfer managers with experiences in development as well as manufacturing, adds tremendous value. If a trans-fer manager knows that he will be intimately involved and responsible with the plant for a successful start-up or launch of a new product, he will also be intimately involved with R&D during development. This role often times may be as simple as explaining why a certain approach taken at the lab scale cannot be done at mass production scale. In return, having experienced members of R&D at the plant level can add significant value with technical details needed in the resolution of many problems. Due to technology, processes, or pending patent designs, you may have an NDA (Non-disclosure Agreement) in place to protect the interest of the company. However, allowing non-disclosure of results between the lab and the plant is disastrous.

Disclosing technical information regarding manufacturing equipment is crucial also. Follow this example and see if it rings a bell. Over the loud speaker comes the following page: "John, come to press #3, it is doing it again."

The plant manager hears the page and calls the production supervisor of the sequence. "Jimmy, why are the press operators always calling John to the problems?"

"Well boss, John is the best we've got on the press, and he can figure it out in no time," responds Jimmy.

"Jimmy, what if John gets run over by a train tonight on the way home, or what if John gets tired of always getting calls at all hours of the night about the presses?" asked the plant manager.

Jimmy does not respond for a moment and seemingly throws in the towel and asks, "Ok boss, whatcha want me to do?"

No doubt this happens all too often in the plant, and at the end of the day, we all want the press back up and running ASAP. The plant manager is right on, though, in that John could leave the company for one reason or the other, and the plant will suffer. Here is an opportunity to work with the maintenance manager to have John transfer knowledge. Now, John may be reluctant to do this in that he likes being the go-to-guy and again feels that having knowledge is power. You need John and he is a valuable member of the team, but John can't run the plant. You must enforce getting others up to speed for multiple reasons mentioned including the need for John to learn more about other equipment in the plant. Failing to strengthen your technical bench is just that - failing.

Avoiding Laundry Lists

The term "laundry list" is believed to have originated in Civil War times. Soldiers would put together a list of their items to be laundered and pray they were returned. This is not unlike our need to list all items we take to the dry cleaners to ensure we come home with the same lot. Through the years the term has come to mean any relatively long, detailed lists of items. Especially long lists associated with negative things, such as complaints. This goes hand in hand with surprises, but have you ever been in a meeting and someone brings up something that just makes you cringe? Granted, there are situations and events not relative to the overall success of the plant that need to be contained, or you become a drama queen. But a lot of times when an area is struggling and continues to go down hill, the poop hits the fan. Meaning in defense mode, they bring out a laundry list of historical problems that need to be resolved. Why did they sit on these problems so long? Could they not get the support needed upstream to help resolve? Did they hope the problems would take care of themselves? YES.

Embedding full disclosure within the plant culture strongly promotes that daily engagement will address the needed issues. It requires excellent communication between shifts, sequences, supervisors, maintenance and operators. It is a "do not pass the buck" mentality that accepts responsibility for the problem at hand. At home we all know too well that if we let the laundry continue to pile up, eventually we have nothing clean to wear. Experience at work should tell us if we continue to let the laundry pile up, our boss will have nothing clean to say.

Like most other key principles of leadership, including humility, integrity, self-discipline, and character, full disclosure is a behavior. Contrary to what some believe, behaviors can be learned and improved to develop greater, overall positive influence on the plant.

10

Guarding Against Presumptions

Presumptions and Assumptions: Putting out the Fire with Gasoline or Water

So you head in to work early this morning because you need to get a jump on things and because, face it – you haven't been sleeping all that well lately. Your performance indicators are not looking good this month, and your downtime is threatening to go through the roof, right along with your boss. The gee-gaw press has really been acting up lately and nobody (not even you!) has been able to solve the core problems with the doggoned thing. Well, at least the manufacturer's technician will be in from Europe in a few days, and maybe you'll be able to salvage the month after he does his magic.

As you pull into the McDonald's drive thru lane to get your first coffee of the day, you wonder why the place is so dark. _NUTS!_ They don't open until 6:00

am. What a great way to start the day. Resigning yourself to dealing with the lack of caffeine, you get back on the road for the remaining ten minutes of the drive.

You drop your briefcase in your office, grab your hard hat and head on out to the gee-gaw press. Before you get within a hundred feet of the press, you know something is wrong – it's way too quiet. Nothing is running! You quicken your pace and turn the corner into your domain and see that not only is the press not running, but there is also nobody there! Where is the operator? Where are the material handlers? *Just what the heck is going on here?!* You walk to the maintenance shop to see if you can find anything out from the night shift mechanics and nobody is there either. Now your blood is beginning to boil. What is it with these people? Don't they know how important that press is? Don't they *care?* You figure that they must be in the lunch room screwing off. They probably do that every night, and you're going to catch them in the act only because you came in three hours early. Sure enough, everybody is sitting around the table in the lunch room drinking that coffee you need so badly. You pause for a moment – just a moment- before you proceed to go ballistic. "Why is everyone just sitting here? It isn't break time!" you yell. "Here I am, three hours early, and I find you all doing nothing while the press is down. What gives?" Your outburst is greeted with dead silence. Looking around, you see some unexpected faces. The day shift mechanics are here four hours before their shift is to start. Without understanding, you notice that the operator and material handlers are sweaty and their clothes are stained with dirt and raw materials. Everyone looks as though they haven't showered in a month. As they all silently shuffles out of the room, ignoring you, you feel your blood pressure continuing to rise as your pulse pounds in your ears. It doesn't take you long to find out what has really been going on, because just as everyone finishes filing out, the night shift supervisor walks in to brief you. The press went down at midnight and the operators and material handlers have been busting their butts trying to get it going. The supervisor woke the day shift maintenance crew to get them in to help, and the supervisor has been on the phone to Europe for two hours trying to get some guidance.

A song lyric begins playing in your head. It's David Bowie and he is singing "…and I've been putting out the fire with gasoline….."

It will take you a long time to recover from your presumption that your people were screwing off and didn't care whether the press was running or not. If you had assumed there was a problem and went about investigating the situation by first seeking out the night shift supervisor, you probably could have avoided the humble pie you are going to eat for the next several months.

Assumptions are essentially educated guesses that you hope are correct. You're willing to modify assumptions as information is gathered. Presumptions are guesses that you take to be the <u>TRUTH!</u> Put even more simply, when confronted with a fiery problem in the factory, assumptions are water while presumptions are gasoline.

If assumptions are educated guesses, from where does that education come? Let's look at a few examples.

You make assumptions each and every day of your life (we all do), and most of 'em are good. You presume the mail will run six days a week, (because that's what the postal service does) and assume that it will arrive in your box at a certain time. You assume that your car will start when you turn the ignition, and that your neighbor's dog will probably leave a deposit on your front lawn at least once a week. But are these truly assumptions? Sure they are, but each is based on different _statistical_ probabilities which predict outcomes.

In the case of the postal service, your assumption the mail will be delivered at 2:00 pm as advertised is based on a long _experience_ of finding mail in your box six days a week at 2:00 pm. And on occasions of an empty box, we bet that your first thought is, "I guess the mail isn't here yet." Your experience leads you to the conclusion that you are suffering nothing more than a statistically insignificant anomaly, and you won't sweat it. _(Bryan – and if corporate headquarters leaves you alone for a whole day, you can consider that a statistically insignificant anomaly as well!)_

Cars are much more reliable these days, so even if you tend to ignore routine maintenance, you have a pretty good shot at the beast starting every day. But since you are a competent factory type who knows how to take care of things, you make sure the battery is always properly charged, the fuel system is clear and clean, and the tank is not empty. Your assumption that the car will start is based on _preparation_ you yourself have performed. A statistical exception that the car won't start will really surprise you.

Your poor lawn is evidence that dogs are dogs, and since your neighbor doesn't keep his tied up, your _observation_ is that sooner or later you are going to have to grab your handy dandy pooper-scooper and clean up a mess....and yet again, trudge over to the neighbor to complain.

So we don't believe that assumptions born of _experience, preparation,_ and _observation_ are bad things or necessarily lead to bad things. Indeed, they are the very basis of how we live our lives, lead our people, and manage our sequences in the factory. Put another way, it's gonna be a long, long day if you have to question each and every assumption you make because you can't trust your experience, preparation and observation. Your mail will run tomorrow; your car will start tomorrow, and just be sure to step over the dog poop instead of in it. If you had to measure each of these events continually, along with the hundreds of other assumptions you are willing to make each and every day, you would need an army of assistants. Without the ability to assume, you won't get much accomplished.

What we do believe, however, is that assumptions made without experience, preparation, and observation are really nothing more than presumptions -buckets filled with gasoline.

Experience

Managers with a lot of years under their belts are prone to remind those around them: *"There is no substitute for experience."* This old proverb can be true, but it depends greatly on the manner in which the experience was obtained. A manager who has been promoted, transferred to other locations, and assumed increasingly, more responsible roles may well have the ability to be right more than wrong. He may also be particularly adept at predicting the human aspects of management as well as negotiating treacherous currents therein His assumptions will have good probability of positive results. A manager who has seen only one location and has performed the same job for twenty years will be an expert in that job but will be unlikely to offer good assumptions outside his arena. There is a difference between twenty years of experience and one year of experience repeated twenty times over. Assumptions of experience are useful in all situations, but most keenly in those dealing with people. That being said, the following is a sample list of situations in which your experience (or soon to be acquired experience) can be relied upon for accurate outcomes:

- Personnel: You know your people (or should) better than any personnel director at the corporate level could ever hope to know. You will be able to lead your personnel group in drafting polices that are effective and predictable. Likewise, you will be able to manage reward and disciplinary situations adeptly.

- Change: Managing changes, large or small, are perhaps the most difficult of management tasks and are best handled by those with experience. As a rule, people resist change, and those most senior resist the most. People are usually brought on board by full disclosure and demonstrate the real need for change. Since change is always effected by the people who are affected, your leadership skills will be paramount here. The message of change can be most effectively delivered by those with experience. Showing your people that you have been there and done that will help, but remember that a bad message delivered well is still a bad message, no matter how experienced you are.

• Culture: Your experience will have exposed you to both good and bad cultures. You will have learned what and what not to do. If you are below the plant manager level, do not be surprised if the plant manager seeks you out for culture questions. Assuming he is not an island unto himself, he will look for those in the organization who can offer good advice. If he is very experienced, he will know he does not have all the answers. If he is not experienced, he may well look for all the help he can get. Beware of the inexperienced manager who doesn't seek counsel, and be sure to offer him yours.

Preparation

"Spectacular achievement is always preceded by unspectacular preparation."
-Robert Schuller

There are people who seemingly accomplish the difficult with little or no effort. The facts are always at their command; questions are answered seamlessly; and all materials needed are there and ready to go. These are managers who have learned the truth of Schuller's quote. They prepare as needed to accomplish the task. You will find both experienced and inexperienced managers who understand the value of planning; the experienced do it because they know planning works, and the inexperienced do it to minimize the effects of their small knowledge base. Many large organizations even devote entire groups to planning, complete with the title of "Planning." Your yearly, plant budgets are plans that have taken a good deal of time and effort to compile. After completion and approval, your budgets are then turned over to corporate where they are combined with many other budgets into a master plan for the entire company. This entire process generally takes up to four months to complete … imagine, one-third of any year is devoted to preparation for the following year. And yet we often find people in our organizations that are willing to act before planning.

Results cannot be spoken into existence, but we are always amazed when this simple reality is ignored. How many times have you witnessed a last minute scramble to correct a bad outcome that should have been avoided long before the rubber met the road? Too often, we are sure. Mistakes of preparation are often the result of presuming a straight, line path to the end goal when reality dictates that the path is more akin to a dog's hind leg – anything but straight. Good preparation involves assuming that bad outcomes are just as possible as good ones and must be accounted for. At the factory level, preparation must often be done quickly and accurately in order to meet deadlines critical to corporate goals. Some guidelines for better preparation:

- If you are a plant manager, state clearly the goal you are trying to reach and exactly why it is important. Do not hold back from honest, open discussion of the possible pitfalls with your team. It is not a bad thing to begin preparation by recognizing where the dangers lie. Your team will be responsible for a lot of the work, so it surely is a good idea to let them know what is going on and encourage them to voice their concerns. Failure of preparation will show up quickly in bad meetings. This is usually in the form of an inability to answer questions correctly and generally just by looking ignorant. We can assure you that your team wants neither.

- Go to the experts. Recognize when you know what you don't know. Unless you are an electrical engineer, it's a doggone good idea to find out how you are going to pull 480 volt power to the new line! We have seen something like this overlooked until equipment was delivered ready for installation, delaying the entire project. Even worse, we have seen instances in which foreign equipment was ordered in the wrong voltage! If the experts are in your building or on your team, so much the better. If not, go get 'em.

- Be critical, both of yourself and your team. Questions of how, why, and when will reveal if your team members have done their homework and are prepared. Of yourself, you should ask "what am I missing?" about a hundred times a day.

- The depth of preparation should match the magnitude of the task. If a task is complex, it may well help to use project management software, Gantt chart preparation, and resource allocation methods. If a task is small and relatively simple, forego the use of these tools. Don't use a shotgun to kill a gnat!

- Document, document, document. Remember that you will forget. CRS disease affects most of us. *(Carl-Shut up, Bryan!)*

- Challenge. Challenge assumptions of which you are suspect. If you are responsible for producing a new product and are told the properties and specifics will be ready when you are, it is not unreasonable to ask for details. While dual-path development isn't uncommon, it requires flawless coordination and timing. Flawless timing and coordination isn't possible if, for example, R&D is unwilling to commit to an end date. If R&D isn't willing to share details of their work, it may well mean that their preparation isn't matching yours. In this case, you will play hell in reaching a good outcome.

We stress, here, that another word for preparation is *"work."* Preparation done well is hard work, and perhaps that explains why many don't do it well, if at all. Be casual in your preparation, and you will gain a deserved reputation as a casual manager. Casual managers don't remain managers for long.

Observation

"*You can observe a lot by watching.*"
—Yogi Berra

Think about it. Yogi was right. In addition, you can't observe without being On the Plant Floor. It is only in this arena in which you gain the *experience* and ability to *prepare.* Ignore that your observations must take place On the Plant Floor, where the action is, and you will ensure that your assumptions (predictions) will result in bad outcomes. Your continual *observations* will form the foundation of your *experience,* and it is where you will learn the importance of *preparation.*

- Watch your people: Observe their actions and interact with them at all opportunities. They will be your teachers, and you will learn much from them. Sometimes you will have good lessons and sometimes bad, but in all cases, you will learn.

- Note any daily abnormalities: The reality is that you will "manage by exception," and it is the differences from day to day that will provide the most information. This is the basis for which control charts are used. The tendency toward drift and change indicates when active involvement is required.

- Experiment: Take the time and effort to "tinker" when it safe to do so and won't affect sequence results. Turning knobs and watching the outcome will not only satisfy your natural curiosity, but will also further your education. Try new things for the sake of trying new things....after all, change is the only constant in your factory and in life.

- Observe your superiors: They will teach you both good things and bad, just as your subordinates will. Catalogue the good; study the bad; and find the path to finding out who you want to be. Remember that bad things may well teach you much more than good things.

- Question everything:

  ✓ Why is the line down so much?

  ✓ Why is there so much starting and stopping?

  ✓ Why is the product temperature varying so much?

  ✓ Why is the third sequence step causing so much scrap?

  ✓ Where is the mechanic/electrician when the line goes down?

  ✓ Where is the supervisor? Why am I by myself out here?

Ask these type questions to yourself and go find the answers. Those answers may come from your people, your boss, your mechanics, or your own hard work, but it is essential that you go about getting them. If your *observations* don't lead you to question the status quo, you will not be able to make the changes that should be part of continual improvement and a part of your culture.

Safety — You did turn that off, didn't you?
There is one area in your factory in which we want you to understand that no presumption should ever be allowed, and that all assumptions must be scrutinized continuously - safety. According to the Bureau of Labor Statistics there were over 800,000 accidents in manufacturing operations in 2009. Think about that. 800,000 recordable accidents! That's 800,000 families affected, 800,000 accident reports, and 800,000 bad outcomes. One area in which you must maintain constant vigilance is safety procedures and conditions which allow accidents to occur. All the experience, preparation, and observation in the world won't sew a hand back on an arm.

"Carl — At a factory in Tennessee that Bryan and I managed, we unloaded raw materials by rail car. In fact, one of the first projects I undertook was to convert expensive truck receiving to less expensive rail receipt. The conversion project went well as we had in place an existing rail spur. After installation of the equipment, we routinely and successfully unloaded rail cars achieving the goals we intended.

The rail spur was on a gentle slope, perhaps 1.5 degrees, and I gave no thought to it whatsoever. After smooth operation of the system for over a year, I was interrupted by the raw materials processing supervisor who breathlessly exclaimed, "We let a rail car get away!" Now this didn't register with me at first. I accompanied the supervisor back to the unloading area where the magnitude of the event struck. We were moving a rail- car when it broke loose and rolled down a slope off of our property. Even the railroad installed and maintained car derailer designed to stop runaways had failed. That was 100,000 pounds of rail car plus 100,000 pounds of raw material rolling down a slope toward the center of town, crossing roads and streets. Adding to the distress was the knowledge that it was 3:00 pm, and the city was full of school buses delivering children to their homes. Bryan and the maintenance supervisor jumped in a truck to follow the path of the car. I notified both the railroad and local police of the event and prayed as I never had. In the end we were most fortunate that the rail car did not strike anything until it hit the end of the line at the rail yard. This is where it impacted another car at 30 miles per hour. Nobody was hurt, thankfully, but damage exceeded $120,000.

My failure in this instance was to <u>presume</u> that the raw material personnel would follow proper safety procedures. My lack of involvement in this area allowed sloppy procedure and easy methods to cause a horrendous accident. It turned out that rather than move the rail car into position with a standard cable puller, a highly manual effort; it was easier to push the rail car with a front-end loader. The driver screwed up and let a car go.... something that would never have happened if the car had been on the pulley and winch puller device. I learned in this incident that you can't underestimate the ability of some to *take shortcuts or overestimate just how dumb some people can be, regardless of any safety policy."*

And so we caution that when safety is involved, there can be no accepting of assumptions arising from experience, preparation, or observation. You must question each and every assumption because life is at stake.

In preparation for this book we revisited the works of many of our professional idols, and among the most prominent of those is Dr. W. Edwards Deming. Perhaps his most famous quote is "In God we trust; all others bring data." We love this quote, for in eight short words, it crystallizes the need to know differences between theory and observation, beliefs and results, and most importantly, the difference between assumption and reality.

If Dr. Deming were alive, he might not approve of data being accepted by virtue of experience, preparation, or observation; but since he noted that success is dependent on management providing an environment in which people can succeed and thrive, we suspect he would approve of our conclusions. Your authors are both certified six sigma belt holders and fully understand the value of data and statistical methods in reaching conclusions. Yet we also understand the value of people's experience, preparation, and observation, which can substitute for reams of statistical data. We believe the biggest value in our six sigma belts is in having additional tools to supplement the assumptions made by our people; and by knowing when to dive deeper and get more data so as to modify those assumptions - completing the education in the "educated guess."

Nevertheless, do not be blinded by presumptions masked as assumptions coming merely from the heart. These "rah-rah" pronouncements will lead with phrases such as "I am willing to believe....", or "My sense is that...." and they will not be backed by the experience, preparation, and observation that will lead to good outcomes. No matter the conviction used in the words or the enthusiasm with which the speaker mouths them, they are hollow and impotent things. They will lead you to bad places where you should not willingly go.

11

Cowboy Up!

Bryan-

I moved to Dallas, Texas, in early in 2007. Coming from a town in West Tennessee of 50,000 people, this was quite a change for my family. I had traveled to and worked in Dallas several times over the years but never for an extended period of time. It did not take me long to catch the Texas fever, and soon I was at a western store looking for my super cool cowboy hat and cowboy boots. Hey, when in Rome... I had heard the phrase "Cowboy Up!" a few times over the years from colleagues and friends in Dallas. There was also a rodeo movie from the early 90s that used the term quite a bit. But being in Dallas, it became something I heard quite often from those around me who worked in the plants but also had farms, horses, cattle, and were, in fact, pretty much real cowboys.

If you look up the phrase in the urban dictionary, yes there is an urban dictionary(1), you will find the following explanations:

1. When things are getting tough you have to get back up, dust yourself off and keep trying.
2. Quit your bitching and be a man. When it gets tough, start playing hard.
3. When faced with a hard chore, it's a shift in attitude from "can't" to a positive "can-do" with confidence and a non-complaining spirit that becomes contagious.
4. Basically, another way of saying "Shut up and take it like a man" or "Quit your whining." The term is derived from the popular image of cowboys being tough, unflinching, uncomplaining, and hard-working.

Granted, this is a term that many might take the wrong way while others may look at you like a mule looking at new gate. It is similar to a statement that we have made several times at different locations and have even put a few signs on the entrance of plant doors that read something like, " CHECK YOUR FEELINGS AT THE DOOR, RUNNING A BUSINESS INSIDE, NOT A DAY CARE CENTER." This can come across as relatively harsh and precipitate the expected reaction that the plant manager is certainly a huge A-hole if not understood in the proper context. Then again, a lot are going to think the plant manager is a huge A-hole anyway - it comes with the territory. Plant managers need also read the sign on the door to be admitted.

"Cowboy Up!" became a part of the culture that we were trying to instill in plants at different locations. It was really a way to let others know we had a no quit attitude and believed there would be a way to adapt and overcome. No matter how bleak the situation seemed, we could find the fortitude to dig in and stay the course. We can count more times than we care to about lying under a piece of equipment day and night thinking, "This is bad, this is really bad." Many times we thought we were down for the count, not for hours but for days, weeks, and possibly months. And you know what? There were those times, but we surrounded ourselves with the right people who had diverse talents and experience and allowed us to work through the issues and get back online.

One example in particular involved - let's say not the most skilled electrician we have ever had on the team. He worked C shift, which usually will include more junior members with less experience. We had a large press in the operation (one of two) that was critical to overall production, quality, and success of a shift. It was a German piece of equipment that either ran flawlessly or did not run at all. A small electrical problem occurred around 2:00 am one night, and it involved a 24v contactor. Unfortunately, the electrician attempted to jump the contactor out and somehow put 480v on the circuit. After the smoke settled, we opened the cabinet doors to a have a look. It was bad … really bad. Wires and components were fried all inside the panel. Frankly, it seemed beyond hope at first, and we fully expected that we would be down for weeks needing parts from Germany as well as expensive German technicians ASAP.

If there ever was a time to Cowboy Up, that was it. Thoughts of calling in the posse quickly came to mind, you know- John Wayne, Johnny Cash, and John Deere. Having one of the two large presses in the plant down for months would obviously cause product shortage. It would increase cost and result in the layoff of half the plant personnel. This was not good for anyone involved, especially the local leadership. We did what we had done over and over for many years: pray and call the most talented people in the plant together to dig in. This involved our maintenance manager, key electricians, and phone support from Germany. It's one of those times when an immediate reaction might be to call corporate and let them know. We talked it over and decided it was best to gather all the details, so we knew what we were up against before notifying corporate. (*This is a good tip on Managing Upstream Expectations – hold your horses!*) With a lot of man-hours involving serious electrical print dissection, parts swapping, and re-wiring, we had the press up and running 8 hrs later. The press was not fully fixed, but it allowed time to develop a long term plan, get parts in, and schedule planned downtime for the work. We were able to maintain production require-ments, hold down costs, and keep people working.

Unquestionably, you have faced many comparable incidents. How do you main-tain forward momentum in tough times like these? How do you convince the troops the battle is not over? How do you as leader, convince others to "Cowboy Up?"

"Cowboy Up" is truly more than a statement. It's a culture, a standard, a way of life that evolves to be the norm - the expected. It is certainly not a time to lose faith, composure, or determination. Whether you are the plant manager, main-tenance manager, or a line supervisor; all around you, people expect you to lead and convey that success is reachable, especially in the face of seemingly unsolv-able problems. It is not a time for panic, berating team members, or creating an expectation of failure. It may, in fact, be time for the *The Walk* we mentioned in an earlier chapter. So utilize this method often if you feel the need, or if a close confidant tells you that you should take *The Walk*. Subordinate the emotion, that's right, forget it and maintain your values.

One of the most important things to keep in mind is that it is *not* a weakness to *not* have an immediate answer for every question. This is critical when dealing upstream with corporate, and it's tough to do. It's very difficult to be a leader (meaning you are in charge) and *not* answer every question put before you. You will influence the culture in a positive way by simply being honest with yourself and your bosses. You can respond that you do not know but can assure that you will find an answer. This allows time to regroup, get others involved, and convey a much better and more accurate response. This does *not* show weakness or incompetence. It shows experience, integrity, and that you are human.

Bryan-

After I was fully indoctrinated with the "Cowboy Up" methodology in Texas, I came back to Tennessee for a short time and met up with some of the old gang from the plant there in Jackson. It did not take me long to get into a conversation with the crew, and to work in my new favorite phase of "Cowboy Up." One of the guys was whining and complaining about his new job, the hours, his boss, his team, and so on; therefore, creating the perfect opportunity to let him know it was time to "Cowboy Up." Of course, it was delivered in a light-hearted and joking manner with someone who still is a good friend. I often still use the phrase in plants today and in this manner. It seems to have a positive impact when others realize how their negative comments may be perceived by others.

We have another favorite saying that we've used quite often, and it seems to go hand in hand with "Cowboy Up." It's a basic and instinctive reaction to the familiar reply of "I do not have time." We accepted a long time ago that whether upstream or downstream, no one really wants to hear this. If you allow this as an excuse, it will erode at the culture you are trying to build or maintain. So a good reaction to, "I do not have time" is "Look around you. The whole world is busy. If we do not find a way to make time, someone else will; and we lose as a plant, as a company, and in this day and age, as a country."

Several years ago, our good friend and colleague, Mr. Silver Cornia, said it in another way: "Sometimes you just have to move your ass." Which again is meant to implant a sense of urgency in the cause - an increased energy level, a renewed drive, an inspired determination, and even more so, the need to be hands on at many times.

Whether you are from Texas or a real Cowboy or not, the need to "Cowboy Up!" and convince others in the plant to do the same will be a frequent event. Let's face it, in manufacturing you typically work many hours, different shifts, weekends, get called in, and confront several problem situations. It's not for everyone, and it's not for the weary. As a leader, your true grit will have to strengthen many others around you.

(1) http://www.urbandictionary.com

1 2

E-Mails are Evil

"*Crackberries have become the unofficial mascot of the Age of Speed, but mind your addition. Research revealed that allowing frequent email interruptions causes a drop in performance equivalent to losing ten IQ points---two and a half times the drop seen after smoking pot." (Statistically Speaking" Computing Canada, June 17, 2005.) - Cited by Vince Poscente's Age of Speed*

It's a brave new world, cowboy. You've got your slick and networked computer on your desk, and when you leave your office you can take that little seven pound wonder right along with you; sure in the confidence that no matter where you travel, there is a Wi-Fi network to access. But wait! That's not all! You also have your handy-dandy Blackberry or iPhone, so even when you leave the office to be

On The Plant Floor, you can reach out and touch anyone in the world with.....an e-mail. You are IN COMMAND! A communicator par excellence! Huzzah!

Nah..... you ain't. You're a prisoner of you own device.

Emails are evil because they waste time – yours and theirs.

- It's easy to sit down and waste your time writing 37 emails to your subordinates, causing them needless work in responding. Would you ask your team 37 questions in a row if they were in front of you? Probably not. Treat instructional emails, or those asking for information, as if they were phone calls or face to face conversations. If you won't make a phone call, don't write the email and don't waste their time.

- Some people send exquisitely crafted e-mails that have obviously taken much effort and time to compose. Careful examination of these 6,000 word wonders often shows the writer is simply letting you know he wants to meet with you at 10:00 AM tomorrow - something he could have told you in a simple phone call.

Emails are evil because they are easy.

- Remember memos and secretaries? *(Carl - Even I don't remember dictation and I'm old). (Bryan – Yes, he is.)* The ease of e-mail communication has eliminated the judgment previously used; it used to take time, effort and people to send written communication, and managers communicated judiciously <u>*because*</u> of the effort required.

- *Emails are evil because they can be the refuge of the lazy.*

- Old style timewasters wandered around the office with a cup of coffee, interrupting those working with idle chit-chat. Now they don't even have to bother to make a pot of coffee to waste time; they can do it from their desk. *(btw... if you have one of those big ole' coffee cups and fill it up often and never make a pot of coffee yourself--- you're a bum!)*

- It's so easy to send an email asking for information you could have gotten by doing a bit of digging by yourself, and you might as well just ask another 36 questions to reach your afternoon quota. This just pisses people off.

Emails are evil because they substitute for personal contact.

- Introverts love e-mails. They *really* love e-mails. *Carl — I once had a new boss whose office was, I swear to you, no more than five feet from mine. Rather than get up from his desk and holler at me, he would send me an email to come to his office right away. For awhile I thought he just didn't like me, but I soon found out he communicated with everybody this way. After several months of this (and other peculiarities), I realized that it was time to execute my out of the organization move. It's always difficult to figure out the best way to initiate these plans, but since he didn't like face to face communications, I simply sent him an e-mail questioning one of his directives. It read, "Your decision defies any logic with which I am familiar." After a day or so, I received an e-mail reply from him berating me for my sarcasm. Of course, he didn't realize I was firing the first shot across his bow; but he was so introverted that even though my message enraged him, he couldn't talk to me face to face.* There are bosses who prefer to communicate by e-mails, and that's fine, so long as electronic messages don't replace "face time" or verbal communication. These are the guys who spend much of their time in meetings and simply can't spend a lot of time on the phone. You will find that even though they prefer you to send emails, they won't burden *you* with their excessive emails.

E-mails are evil because they hinder problem solving and news of important events.

- If you have ever had a minor disaster and were tempted to send the news to your boss by e-mail, then don't. At best you will be seen as hiding behind your keyboard, and at worst, your message will be misunderstood - perhaps even magnified well beyond the true impact on the organization. Pick up the phone and make the call; if you must, follow with an email.

- We have rarely seen plant problems solved by a flurry of e-mails. Factory problems are solved by face to face communication *and moving your ass.*

Just as you can't turn a wrench while sitting at your desk, you can't solve problems from there, either. Problem solving and forward progress require engagement, not e-mail messages back and forth between your people. If you have fallen into the trap of the 37 e-mails, you may well find that your people dread opening up their inbox. Your effectiveness will be diminished and the culture damaged.

E-mails are evil because they are no more than electronic dots on a screen.

- Don't underestimate the effect a poorly worded, punctuated, or seemingly innocent e-mail you send can have on those who read it. You will not be there to nuance the words or gage the response of the recipient. A simple phrase like "Why has the gee-gaw press broken down?" can be interpreted by the reader to be "Why the #@$% has the gee-gaw press screwed up again? What the *&%# are you guys doing down there??!!"

- Don't underestimate the effects a nasty e-mail can have on you. *Carl – During a stressful start-up, I began to receive emails from my boss that showed he was jumping to conclusions about relatively minor matters. They were not related to our goal of bringing the plant on line, in time and within budget. These emails were of a particularly nasty nature revealing his stress levels. Knowing that he was wrong in his conclusions and way out of line; I telephoned him, and in no uncertain words, told him how upset I was with his e-mail. I let him know it would have been far simpler and easier on both of us if he had picked up the phone to discuss it. I am not prone, these days, to anger easily, but he had gotten to me, and he certainly did not get the reaction he expected or wanted.*

- Some people read exclamation points and hear screaming, even when not meant. This is particularly true for people for whom English is a second language. If you hear screaming when you read exclamatory sentences, pick up the phone, and call the writer and ask what is going on. You may find the exclamation point wouldn't have been there if written in Chinese, or you may find out the writer really was screaming. Either way, you find out.

E-mails are evil because they can be sent to so many people.

- Have you ever received a mass distribution e-mail from the corporate head-quarters that was addressed to all people in the company? If you have, then you have probably snickered at all the people who responded to it by click-ing "respond to all". You can generate one helluva lot of emails this way.

- If you have legitimate need for information or wish someone's opinion on a matter that can't be handled in face to face communication or by phone call (long distance!), don't copy the world on it. Your boss doesn't need to know you are talking to Bill about a problem, and Bill's boss doesn't need to know. Copying superiors on emails leads people to believe you are pres-suring them to deliver something "or else!" Keep your e-mails addressed to those with legitimate concern in the matter. *Legitimate* concern is dif-ferent from *casual* concern. Should you not learn this lesson, there may be a name attached to your reputation that politely can be translated to part chicken and part what the dog left you in the yard.

- If you constantly BCC (blind courtesy copy) people in your messages, refer to the closing of the above bullet point.

Emails can be great for sharing data, presentations, documents, etc. They're a great time and money saver; use them when you can't use anything else, or when you legitimately need to document events and actions. HOWEVER, do not use e-mails and your 9,468 folders as though you worked for CSI. Using your investigative search skill to find old e-mails to argue points with people will rarely gain anything more than making you feel better -and smell bad. Refer to previous bullet point.

Preferred order of communication

1. Face to face. Always the best, if possible.
2. Telephone. Not quite as good as #1 but an order of magnitude better than #3.
3. E-mail, fax, text messages.

Notice that the order of preference is in inverse proportion to the age of the technology. Of course, face to face communication is the oldest, and it is pre-ferred as it gives the best chance for real, accurate and effective communication.

People can become amazingly bold and brash when sitting at a keyboard and will break all bounds of common courtesy and sense, yet these same people become almost as amazingly, common sensical in person or on the telephone. Just remember – don't send emails that smell like your shoe that just discovered (again) where the dog left you a surprise. Like the dog, you might find your nose rubbed in it later.

Finally, remember that you are in control of your motor skills......your finger. Should you receive one of those smelly emails and angrily begin to respond in kind, remember the best key on the board. That key is "DELETE." Someone gutless enough to send a smelly e-mail is beneath your dignity, so simply get the email out of your inbox, your trash and your life by pressing that wonderful key. It'll do you good, and the sender will likely never bring it up. If he didn't have the guts to telephone with the message, he isn't going to call you to follow up.

Happy e-mailing!

13

The Bean Counters

Like It Or Not – You Need Them

Do you ever feel like your hands are tied, and that you cannot make the decisions needed because of your accountants or controllers? Do they constantly submit to you this code, that accounting principle, or some new, corporate policy preventing you from doing what you think is best? Yep, and it's all part of the operating environment in today's manufacturing plant that helps keep us and the company out of serious trouble. However, are there times when you feel more policed than supported? Is their job even to support the plant anymore since 99% of them report to someone at the corporate office? Here we will discuss some of our lessons earned in regards to developing a productive, working relationship with the finance group – otherwise known to many of the manufacturing team as the "bean counters."

The Sarbanes-Oxley Act came about in 2002 as a reaction to a number of major corporate and accounting scandals including Enron and several others. Sarbox or *SOX*, is a United States federal law that sets new and enhanced standards for all U.S. public company boards. It is named after the sponsors of the bill U.S. senators Paul Sarbanes and Michael G. Oxley. It created new agencies such as the Public Company Accounting Oversight Board charged with overseeing, regulating, and inspecting accounting firms in their roles as auditors of public companies. There is still much debate, and heartburn, over the perceived benefits of *SOX*. Supporters say that it is one of the most needed and far reaching reforms since the FDR days. (Most of these were unemployed accountants now with *Sox* jobs.) Opponents of the bill insist that it has reduced our competitive edge to compete on an international level due to the regulatory and cost requirements for U.S. firms. What does all this mean for you at the plant? An "enlightened" self-sense of responsibility from the finance group that directs the methods of how you expense items, calculate unit cost, and manage inventories.

At times it can seem that the paranoia of all the regulations is to the point that some in the finance group are screaming, "We are all going to die!" or "We are all going to jail!" Keep in mind that the penalties are steep for not following the regulations, and you could earn a quick exit, or worse, if you do not cooperate. Accountants are not the only group that keeps local management out of serious trouble. HR, environmental, and safety personnel also play a critical role in keeping the plant in compliance. Here are a few examples of what happens when the local management breaks the rules:

- *5 members of a meatpacking plant's management team were indicted on 12 counts of charges ranging from immigration-related offences to banking fraud. – Iowa Independent May, 2008*

- *Plant Managers face prison time for covered up oil spill. – The News-Herald (Detroit) July, 2009*

- *Managers of Cheese plant sentenced for theft of thousands of dollars that shut down local factory. – Topeka Capital Journal, April 2002*

- *Managers charged over death of plant worker that was instructed to increase the amount of sodium hydrosulfide to speed up a wastewater treatment process. A chemical reaction occurred and killed the worker. – Chemical Insider Daily – Hamilton, OH, June 2010*

- *Plant Manager faces charges of stealing. A plant manager of an herb company indicted for writing checks to family members for work not performed. Her husband was taking payments for a maintenance business unrelated to the plant. — NBC4i — Claremont, NH August 2010*

Perhaps you're thinking, "Well those are just criminal, gross negligence and incompetence examples that I or my staff would never be involved in." Here are few more examples.

- *Plant Manager charged with trade secrets theft. A plant manager of more than 20 yrs retired from an electrical transformer company and years later joins another company were he divulged proprietary information. — Womble Carlye Attorneys — Conway, SC December 2009*

- *NY Coke Plant and Environmental Manager Charged. Both were charged for criminal activities related to violating federal clean air laws. The pollution control baffles on their exhaust stacks were found not to be operating properly and they knew about it. They did not want to spend the company money to fix due to the cost on the plant. — Associated Press Aug. 2010*

- *Former plant manager of recycling plant sentenced. He reportedly received over $30,000 from a person hired to transport materials from the transfer station to the incineration facility. — Associated Press, June 2010*

- *Plant Manager sentenced for 78 months. The manager joined the company in an effort to help his father solve the plant's problems. He instructed employees to clean up and get rid of waste. He did not tell them to illegally dump it. At the trial, co-workers stated that the manager was "young and in way over his head." — Brunswick, GA News, January 2001*

- *These guys were nuts! Four local managers faced fraud charges for using their positions to steal and divert nuts from almond growers and sold the nuts on their own. — Turlock Journal — Turlock, CA, August 2010*

As you can see, there is a lot that can go on behind the scenes in manufacturing plants, and unfortunately, policing is required. From these examples, take to heart that as a manager, you are ultimately responsible for all actions of the plant and its workers -good and bad.

If you are a manufacturing manager and get along well with your controller, you are perhaps in the minority, and be thankful for your situation. Let's address some methods on improving the working relationship between the two groups recognizing that common goals should dutifully represent the company well.

Due to some of the regulatory changes, like *SOX*, most controllers report to a financing director or VP at the corporate office. This is understandable to avoid conflicts of interest, such as the local plant manager potentially instructing the controller to make decisions that could impact his salary or his good standing with the boss. You will have to work hard at forming a productive relationship with your controller. This doesn't mean you have to like each other – you probably won't.

One tip is to make time (agreeable to both) daily to meet and update each other on any new topics. From the plant manager's side, it could be production status, expenditures, and any relative talks with corporate. From the controller's side, it could also be talks with corporate that impact the plant, cost status, or changes needed. Lack of *communication* is always one of the sources of failures for any relationship and is especially true in this case. Meeting each day will avoid surprises on both sides and will allow collective forecasting to be more accurate.

Another tip is to make sure you maintain good relations with the *controller's boss*. This is not to be an underhanded approach but an effort to defuse any misunderstandings between the plant and corporate. If your controller's boss likes and respects you, it is unlikely he will allow the controller to lay blame solely upon the plant management. The responsibility for missing financial forecasts should always be shared between finance and manufacturing.

Learn to value the controller's input (hard as it may be) and ask for it often. Getting their buy-in on management decisions, changes, and the implications for cost creates *unity*. Like many decisions at the plant level, not all are black and white when spending is involved. Should I spend the money now or later? How will this purchase impact the plant and monthly statements? You need the controller's input and advice on these and other matters. There are times when you make a decision that the controller may not agree with, but you must still keep them informed. Fundamentally, you are responsible for the plant and will make the best decision you can with the information at hand. If that means that you have to take a hit on the financial side when it is still best for the plant and company long term, you will make it.

Company Policy or Personal Policy?

One of our experiences involved a few changes of the guard on the finance side. Our company merged with another company, and of course, the new company thought the old company was whacked. New finance leaders were involved, and soon it became obvious that one of the goals was to take the private company public. Within two years this happened, and our accounting practices changed forever. A few years after the company went public, it was purchased by a much larger corporation. Again, we experienced many leadership changes on the finance side in particular and new policies quickly emerged.

As we all know, empire building is a reality in the business world, and finance is not immune. As certain groups gain more power, it becomes clear which ones have more influence over the company as a whole. If the core leadership group is "boots on the ground" manufacturing executives that built the company from ground up, they will lean toward being more manufacturing friendly. If the current executive groups have more of a sales background, you got it; sales will get more attention and funding.

In our case, we went through a changing of the guards that involved the CFO being promoted to CEO. Did the accountants and controllers experience head swelling? You bet, so we quickly began to see the demands shift on the corporate needs. More weekly reports concerning finances, tighter budgets, and expectations of improved inventory turns immediately were enforced. It seemed that each week our controller would inform us of something we needed to change or complete by the end of the day. We did our best (most of the time) to meet the terms of the demands, but it soon came to a head as we began to see that our local controller had personal policy instead of corporate policy. "No, you can't do this, or you must do that," grew old quickly, so we began to push back and ask for copies of the supposed policies that instructed us in such a manner. In many cases, there was no policy- just simply a difference of opinion on how to handle certain issues; but since the finance group had leverage at the top, we remained under an iron first. Yet we knew this situation had to be improved, or the plant and company would suffer the most. It became even more apparent when a performance evaluation gave us very bad marks on communications with the finance group.

Coming Out The Other Side

In our case, we constantly felt handicapped with limited cost information and lack of forward visibility to help make the best decisions. We were getting hammered from the manufacturing and finance, executive side over missed indicators. Numbers from the finance group had not been good; the plant labor costs were rising, and production volumes had too much fluctuation. Scheduling changes, product mix, new product launches, and increased waste were the culprits, but when cost are out of line, what difference does it make? A lot, *if* you can get your controller to support and show the details to back-up the statements. This would require a much finer-grained understanding of the many components of product costs. From what we knew was taking place on the plant floor, we felt the numbers would recover over the next quarter from improvements made in scheduling, product mix, and new product stability. The executives did not care about all the details involved; *fix the problems now*. We worked closely with our controller to improve our forecasting accuracy, and soon the variance was back in line.

As difficult as the situation was, it did further our ability to gather data and improve financial decisions. Here are a few changes that came from those experiences:

- Monthly raw material inventories were changed to weekly.

- Cycle counts for finished goods and the tool-crib were increased to quarterly instead of bi-annually.

- We worked with the controller to do a bi-monthly, soft, internal closing before the end of the month hard closing to improve forecasting.

- Our weekly conference calls with corporate included the controller, and we required that he give input.

- We worked with the controller to run constant new scenarios on labor changes, capital expenditure justifications, and raw material substitutions to learn the impact on cost.

- We took a crucial step forward from manufacturing side and started approving standard cost of all SKUs.

These changes were significant in both improvements needed for the plant and relations between the manufacturing team and our controller. A plant with several SKUs often finds that fixed cost for capital equipment and inventory charges are spread across the SKU groups, masking changes in variable cost. When products are scrapped as obsolete, it could be from poor, sales' forecasts by marketing. These scrap numbers should show up in productivity, but since multiple products pass through the same production lines and share the same workers, the averaging distorts the true cost picture. Volume and mix swings accentuate this type of a problem. Finally, when this takes place, changes in output volume may not see cost follow; likewise, as there is a lag in consuming inventory. Developing an understanding for these type scenarios certainly requires assistance from your controller. Coming through the fiery trials improved our skills on the finance side and allowed us to be more well-rounded managers.

The term "bean counter" is most used in a negative sense. It does appear that plant managers and accountants come from different planets and are at odds a great deal. However, both are clearly critical functions in the manufacturing plant. Our strong recommendation is to work hard on improving communications, involvement, and overall relations with your controller. Your capacity to become much more astute on finances is essential for plant and personal development. Further more, it's good to audit the auditors. You need to know what's all in the numbers and count the beans yourself.

14

Managing Upstream and Downstream

Swimming with the Sharks

As far as we are concerned, the worst job in the world is plant manager. Who, given the opportunity, to pick his dream job will pick the one in which he must satisfy both those above him and those below him without disappointing either? It may be the worst job in the world, but it is one both of us have had, held and loved. If you are there, you will go home at night wondering why the heck you agreed to take on this responsibility ... and the answer is clear ... this is _what you do._ You can't explain why you do this anymore than we can explain why we have done it. Like it or not, this is who you are, what you do, and what you have been called to do as a manufacturing manager. Nobody, who hasn't been there, will understand why you are willing to take on more than anyone else you know, but you do. Between explaining to those above you who question your decisions and understanding to those below you who ask the same questions; you will need to swim with the sharks more often than you sleep in your own bed. Our hats are off to you, plant manager, because we have walked a mile in your shoes.

Managing downstream is easy to understand. You are in charge of a sequence or a plant; your title is manager or supervisor; and in the typical pyramid org chart, you have people underneath you. Managing upstream is a bit harder to grasp, but you were actually born with this ability. Ever been in a toy store and see a kid scream, plead, and cry until the parents, out of exhaustion, buy the toy the little darling wanted? You have just witnessed a well-developed ability to manage upstream. There certainly are overgrown children in the manufacturing world, and you've probably witnessed more than a few screaming fits by these managers; you've also probably greeted their replacements! Well, we will assume you're on your meds and could use some practical guidance. It is striking that while there are countless places you can find information on managing downstream (leadership), there are few sources of information for swimming in the opposite direction.

Managing "upstream" is really managing expectations - you can't really *direct* your boss (or their boss, for that matter), but you *can* interact with them in a way in which they learn to react predictably to you and events in your area. In other words, you can guide them to see things as you do. Some might see this as manipulation, but is that so bad? If your "guidance" leads to forward progress and/or reduction of effort and fosters continuous improvement, then manipulation in the name of effectiveness is a *very* good thing. The vision of the promised land is enough to convince others to make the journey, and you must lead the way.

Managing Upstream Guide

- You have preferences for the way people communicate with you. You might be a "phone" guy; you might be an "email" guy. If you don't know how your boss likes his communication, then ask him. He will be more than happy to give you the answer, and you might well have the pleasure of him asking you the same thing. While you are asking him how, also ask him when. There are certain things you will *always* need to report. These include natural disasters, legal and regulatory violations, and major events. Beyond that, it will come down to an agreement between the two of you as to when you need to initiate communication. You won't know when that will be unless you ask him, and you will definitely come in for criticism if you communicate either too much or too little. You may not find perfect, communication frequency out of the box, but you will never find it without his input. For example, if you over-communicate without immediate response, you may find yourself constantly frustrated and then later chagrinned to find out your boss only reads emails once a day and is wondering why the heck you sent him 10 emails. (BTW, how do you find time to send 10 emails when you should be ON THE PLANT FLOOR?)

- Attitude is important. Concentrate on the ideas or directives rather than who is delivering them. Not all your directives will come from your boss. They may come from corporate personnel, safety, or accounting groups. Your attitude with them – good or bad – will get back to your boss and help or hurt you. Ask questions in a neutral, unthreatening way. Don't let your first question be "What genius thought this up?"

- If you are having trouble implementing a corporate directive, document the problems with data instead of emotion. Most management will understand, "We attempted the super-slick, double-bend adjustment last night, and after tweaking the line over two hours for optimum performance, we found our reject rate climbing to 80%." They will also understand YOU are a pain in the arse if you state "Well, we tried that crap, super-slick double-bend adjustment last night, and it was a flaming disaster. Told you so!"

- Be a "maybe" man. You know "yes" man is a polite term for being gutless. Just as bad is a "no" man who gives immediate and negative answers, always arguing against ideas. A "no" man shouts to all that he is smarter and more capable than his boss and has little regard for the position of others. Between these two extremes is the "maybe" man. Avoiding immediate answers (if he is unsure), he signals to those upstream that he will consider all opinions and respond appropriately. The "maybe" man will cover a lot of middle ground, sometimes closer to "no" or "yes," but rarely occupies either extreme.

- Know when to hold 'em and know when to fold 'em. You must be certain whether a reportable issue is really an issue. This will require patience on your part and trust in your team to avoid "crying wolf." Jumping to conclusions or reporting events – good or bad – before enough evidence is in for confirmation will damage your credibility. A manager can repair many different kinds of missteps, but he can't recover from a non-credible label.

Job Scope

You are gonna make dozens of decisions each day. It's likely you will make them all by your lonesome without seeking approval. This makes you captain of your fate. Lord knows, there are few people who want to take the reins from your hands. You are in control.

The realization that you largely control your job scope is one of those "light-bulb" moments too few managers experience, yet this understanding is important for those who want to be effective both upstream and downstream. What? Determine my own job scope? No, we aren't crazy.

Unless you are in a newly created position, you are following in another's footsteps. Since you are a different person than your predecessor, you will act differently. You will do things in a different manner, have different ideas, and approach problems from a different direction. Shazam! You are defining your job scope.

Simple reality dictates that you don't have total freedom. You can't make the sun rise in the west; you can't break the law without consequences; you can't defy company policy without bringing down your boss's wrath. That's about it. Once you understand you are largely in control of your fate, you will find that your ability to manage both upstream and downstream is greatly enhanced. By leaning out unnecessary reports, phone calls, and emails, you will gain time needed to respond appropriately to the demands placed on you by _both_ upstream and downstream folks.

Managing Downstream Guide –Managing change

- Helping others to understand the need for change is worth the time and trouble it takes. Stick to the business of the matter instead of emotions. As a general rule, people hate change, but you knew that. Remember that you lead people, and you are a leader whether you like it or not.

You are not obligated to do anything that is illegal or unsafe, nor should you allow your people to do so. Outside of that, you are going to have to change things on a pretty regular basis. Don't say, "Do This!" rather say, "We need to do this, and here is why." If you've built a culture of trust and disclosure, the change will go down relatively easily.

• If you can quantify the need for a change, do so. Explaining to people that a sequence is falling behind the output required to feed the next sequence by 48% is understandable. Implementing change by stating they are too slow will probably not get a good result. Stress the rate and how it affects the rest of the plant, not the speed of the employee.

• If you can't quantify the need for change (improved housekeeping, say), implement the change by explaining the need in terms of safety, pride, cleanliness, and plain, old, common sense. Show people your commitment to change by bending over yourself to pick up trash or grabbing a broom to clear a path through the mess. Your willingness to actively participate in a change is worth more than a ten thousand word speech, and it's more fun for your folks, too.

• Difficult implementations are those that are not obvious improvements and come from an imagined, ivory, tower corporate headquarters. Avoid the "Into the valley of death rode the 600" speech by explaining the need as it was explained to you. If you didn't get any explanation yourself, then you have bigger problems than a new directive! Above all, do not direct people by stating you disagree with it but have been ordered to do it. It's tempting to blame things on upper management, but doing so sends the message that:
   ○ You have no spine.
   ○ You are unimportant in the chain of command and are ineffective.
   ○ You are willing to tear down the culture your team is building that says, "We are doing the right thing for the company, and we represent the plant."

Here we reinforce that the worst job in the world is that of plant manager. As arbitrator between corporate needs and your people's needs, you must negotiate a path that will lead all to what is in the best interest of the enterprise. It is a tough place to be, and only the willing can occupy the space.

If you look at the upstream folks and contrast them with the downstream folks, you will see they each want the same thing from you. They want you to be honest, competent, and fair. The difference in dealing with the two groups is more a matter of technique than substance, and understanding that each group must be communicated with in different manners is the key to swimming with the sharks and not getting eaten.

15

Are You An Artist?

Painting the Big Picture

Often we hear that you must look at the big picture, the overall good, and consider the best, long term actions for the organization as a whole. From the manufacturing plant side, conveying a message from your superiors can often be confusing to or misunderstood by the troops in the field. Thus, consider your ability to clarify and paint the big picture or reduce the message down to smaller pictures, that when viewed together, complete the full canvas.

Let's break this down into a specific example that you have faced if you have even a little, manufacturing experience.

Reduce cost now!

If you do not hear this at least once a week, then your Ops VP is on vacation and has the cell turned off. The mandate often comes down as a reaction to many conditions including missed indicators from monthly reports by the entire company, but also can be directly related to the plant's performance. A common reaction is for the plant manager to call all the local management team together to discuss problems and solutions. Prior to calling this meeting, a method that we have found very productive is to make time with an established and respected #2 in the plant (operations manager, assistant plant manager, production manager, etc.) and put together a list of opportunities with his/her strong input and support.

As we will mention often in various chapters, *Unity* is a powerful tool. One objective that should be achieved from developing a key, opportunities list between the plant manager and the #2 manager is to create the same type *Unity* for the entire management team. This ensures that the message delivered to the plant floor is consistent, well thought through, and is without disparity. The list will frequently involve items such as waste reduction, labor reduction, overtime reduction, productivity increases, process flow improvements, and other means to increase positive variation for the plant.

Ok, so you and your #2 are hammering out the details to present to the rest of the management team. Here are some key characteristics of a strong #2, as this is a critical position that should include a strong enough leader who can push back on the #1 when needed. Speaking frankly, in our experience as both #1 and #2, this can be quite often.

The meeting between the two should be behind closed doors. It is often best to have the meeting off site since many times others will see them together behind a closed door and assume the worst. Let's face it, the plant manager is constantly pulled and torn in so many different directions that his finger may not be on the pulse of the plant near as much as the #2. Here's some food for thought #2: Do you spend at least 75% of your time *On The Plant Floor?*

Having the #2 provide key input and collaboration on the opportunities list is critical for the plant as a whole. Check your feelings at the door, argue out the details, get loud, challenge each other, and battle it out. When you are through, open the door, and leave in *Unity.* If you allow others to see tension or contradiction between these two key positions, you will lose much momentum for continual growth. The genuine loyalty and respect between the plant manager and the #2 are essential. This is a core issue in developing the unique, artistic abilities needed to paint the small and large pictures within the manufacturing environment clearly without distortion.

Now back to the list. In this example, the plant manager and #2 zero in on two key sequences that provide the most opportunity for cost reductions. We will also discuss in *Chapter 18 (Spreading The Pain)*, why we have found that labeling areas within the plant as *sequences* instead of *departments* can improve process flow greatly.

Ironically enough, both of the problem sequences are on the same off-shift that runs M-F from 3-11 pm. These sequences also report to the same shift supervisor. Knowing this, and not to create a public persecution for the shift supervisor, we suggest bringing this supervisor into the discussion early in the process. Giving a supervisor a heads up on what will take place in the group, management meeting should be the norm. It shows both direct concern for the supervisor as well as common courtesy and respect by asking for their suggestions and support for the improvements needed.

Prior to bringing in the shift supervisor, the plant manager and the #2 discuss openly if there is a leadership problem on the off-shift with the supervisor involved. If this is the case, the meeting might involve changes within the group to add more support to the off shift in areas of maintenance, quality, engineering, other supervisors, or senior operators. It could also mean that the plant manager and/or the #2 have to spend more time on this shift, as it seems to fall apart later in the night than earlier.

Whether it takes all of the mentioned resources or some of them, make sure that the shift supervisor has a voice and a role in this improvement effort. Ultimately they have the most to gain or lose. If this is a reoccurring problem involving the same shift and supervisor, a change in leadership may be inevitable.

You should be tracking all the obvious indicators and looking to the data for directions, BUT you and your team should also be engaged in the operation at a level that the data only supports and reinforces what the entire team knows is taking place daily *On The Plant Floor* .

The first problem sequence involves:

Raw Material Batching

- Consistently plagued with unplanned downtime

- Carries the highest manpower

- Operates with excessive overtime

- Soaring with high waste

- Frequent turnover of operators

Now that you have reviewed the data and gained the confidence and support of the shift supervisor, he identifies some specific issues in the raw material batching sequence. One of the three mixers on the shift is constantly experiencing electrical downtime. The supervisor's feedback, along with the downtime report, states that electrical downtime is the highest occurrence each night on this shift. However, a report stating one thing and the actual being another is an area you will have to enforce full disclosure on constantly. Does the data match the actuals?

You discuss the data in detail with the shift supervisor, and it is mentioned that a programming issue is allowing more inexperienced operators to constantly get the mixer out of step. This, in turn, creates excessive downtime and waste to the mixer area and to the surrounding auxiliary equipment as well. The supervisor has discussed this with the maintenance staff several times and has also discussed it with the maintenance manager.

Next step? Show the same respect to the maintenance manager that you showed to the shift supervisor and call him in prior to the group, management meeting for his input and support. The maintenance manager quickly recognizes that he does not have the resources or talent on the off-shift to handle the programming needs. He assures all involved that someone with the skills needed from the day-shift crew will be moved promptly to the off shift to work through the issues. Of course, this decision was made after a lengthy debate of how the operators are not trained or qualified well enough on the equipment, or problems would not be happening repeatedly on the same shift. Granted, the maintenance manager has made a good point. After further review of the downtime data on all shifts, it is obvious that this mixer does not only have issues on this shift, but also on others as well, just not as frequently. That said, the shift supervisor agrees to rotate more experienced operators to work with the electrician in order to get to the bottom of the programming issues. As you all know too well, managing conflict between production, management, and maintenance will be areas that consistently require much of your time. If you do not manage these well and put the right players in these critical positions, you will lose many battles and downtime will continue to escalate without resolution.

Now with the support of the shift supervisor and maintenance manager regarding the raw material sequence issues, let's take a look at what's happening in the next problem sequence.

Production line #4

- Low production volume

- Downtime not reported as high

- Waste not reported as high

What? Low production but downtime and waste are in line? I think we've all been here before. The plant manager and the #2 now discuss with the shift supervisor and the maintenance manager the concerns with line #4. Knowing the productivity issues from this line, the maintenance manager is well prepared and shows supporting data that very few calls or actual downtime is reported from each shift. The shift supervisor does not have a good grasp on the specifics with line #4, other than a junior crew has been attempting to run, for several weeks, one of the more difficult products in the plant. What caused this issue? High order rates requiring more lines to run this difficult product, poor production planning or scheduling, order incompletion on first shift, or some other cause? If you do not have an immediate answer for these questions, you've got it; bring in the production scheduler and/or the production manager.

In this case, the #2 is in constant communication with scheduling and is able to reassure the group that orders are high for this product, and multiple shifts are required. It is stressed that we should take hold of a great situation with increased orders and not lose the opportunity to supply the customer base, or someone else will pick up the ball where we dropped it.

Frankly, with all the discussion of the several elements involving line #4, it appears the crew on B shift for this line is not getting the job done. Back to hard and direct questions for the shift supervisor. Hard questions are much easier and *accepted as expected* and fair when you have again developed a culture of constant disclosure without fear of retaliation.

The shift supervisor makes several suggestions for improvements including rotating operators from other lines that have more experience. While this might seem like an obvious approach, weaker leaders find this can be quite disruptive for the operators and the plant -especially if an existing environment allows operators to feel they are dedicated solely to a specific line or machine. Often you might hear chatter such as, "I work on line 3 and run machine 12; it's mine, and I do a great job." While this may very well be true, you must establish a basic foundation that the company, the plant, and local management own and are in charge of the lines and equipment. Make the decisions necessary day in and day out to optimize their use.

Now that the key management group involved has discussed the opportunity areas and planned for changes that lead to improvement, you are ready to deliver, in *Unity, this* message to the rest of the plant management staff.

In our experience, this meeting should include the plant manager, operations manager, production supervisors, maintenance manager, personnel manager, quality control or lab, and someone from scheduling. This core group will brainstorm more regarding the issues with the raw material sequence and production line #4, and more than likely, create more positive changes to the areas involved. These meetings are essential at times and must always be driven by an agenda and a need to keep the meeting length restricted to one hour. It is not a gripe session or an avenue for an individual or sub-group to air a laundry list of issues in their own personal world. Again, if a culture has been established that constantly encourages full disclosure, laundry lists will be minimized.

Now we have the final opportunities list that involves the raw material batching sequence and production line #4.

Raw material batching:

- Move a more skilled electrician with programming skills from day shift to B shift to observe and make needed changes to mixer #3.

- Move a more experienced operator to work with the electrician on mixer 3 in order to quickly resolve the productivity issues involved. During this move, the more experienced operator will spend time helping to develop the less experienced operators on the off-shift as well.

- From the management staff meeting, the lab showed data that the lack of batch consistency from mixer #3 causes quality issues into other sequences. This creates added waste and downtime to the plant as a whole. With this data, the nail in the coffin was driven to all involved concerning the urgency of the turn around needed on B shift regarding mixer #3.

- Agree to follow up toward the middle of the week to review and remove any obstacles that might be preventing the needed progress.

Production line #4:

- Production operators will be rotated from lines with more seasoned operators to run the difficult product that continues to be scheduled for line #4.

- Less experienced operators will work on other lines running similar products and will gain the needed training from other, more experienced supervisors and operators.

- From the management staff meeting, production scheduling indicated that the backlog was not decreasing, and in fact, another line on the off-shift would need a changeover to this product line also. This is a great event for the plant in many ways, but it creates new challenges; and discussion develops around the core issues of what makes this product more difficult to produce than others.

This will require a follow up meeting. The plant manager encourages the production supervisors to get together *On The Plant Floor* during the next run of this product and perform a thorough autopsy on problems at hand and develop an action item list. This list may very well require capital and engineering changes since multiple lines are involved. The plant manager ensures the group that he will support and drive their decisions forward and again encourages the group to deliver in *Unity* the urgency and motives for the changes within the plant.

While this example may seem elementary and Manufacturing 101, often we miss the need for a basic foundation and culture that creates an environment which encourages linear engagement from all. If you are not a great artist, break the picture down into segments that do not seem so abstract that others have to constantly guess at what the big picture really looks like. Do not expect all of the team to be constantly focused on the big picture. There may only be a select few within the management group that will be able to see this. A majority will depend on *you* to show them each day bigger pieces on the canvas. Handle the brush and your strokes wisely as many anticipate the unveiling.

16

Building The Culture

We hear a lot about culture in our society today and are counseled by many to understand different religions, heritages, and ethnicities. We are not here to address these issues in a general way. We will be plant specific and we warn: Ignore the factory culture at your peril.

Regionalism

Notwithstanding the homogenization of America to the point where a Big Mac in New Jersey is identical to one in Montana, there are distinct differences in our nation.

Carl-

I never heard of "Yankee Memorial Day" until I managed a factory in North Carolina. It was common not to observe Memorial Day holiday in this area, as it was believed to be a day celebrating the Union CivilWar victory. Conversely, Good Friday was held sacrosanct as a holiday in the South, while largely ignored as a holiday in northern and western states. Good or bad? Doesn't matter....you just need to be aware of it.

Swearing and bad language is never a good idea, but it is tolerated in many parts of the nation however, don't swear in the presence of a woman in the south. It is highly offensive - plus she might give you the cussin' of your life right back at you!

These are just two examples of the many regional differences in our country. Sometimes the cultural variations will not be obvious. If you are new to an area, take the time to acclimate yourself to the surroundings. Remember, in the south #3 belongs to Dale Earnhardt, not Babe Ruth.

Nepotism

As a new supervisor in a new location, you should pay particular attention to how many people are related. Despite active, anti-nepotism rules in many companies, other firms actively encourage families to work in the same facility in the belief it will foster plant unity. Even after years of working in both conditions, we really don't know if it brings unity; but the obvious danger is that if you offend one, you offend many in the family-populated factories.

Don't get us wrong, we are not discouraging hiring family members. In fact, we have seen this in many cases to be very successful, since family peer pressure can often have more influence than management. Let's say you have a good operator who wants you to hire his brother. This operator has mentioned that he would like to be considered for a supervisor position in the future as well. You can bet this operator will give his brother more crap on and off the field about doing a good job than any other member of management would dare.

Husbands and wives at the same plant are a different story. Far too often you hear of certain situations considered inappropriate in the plant. You've got it, affairs between so and so. It can become your very own soap opera in an area that creates way too much drama for productivity.

Bryan-

I was supervising a night shift sequence when it became all too obvious that Joe from line 2 and Betty from line 3 were becoming way too friendly. They were spending a lot of time chatting, taking their breaks together, leaving for lunch together, and requesting to work overtime together. Well, Betty's husband, Bubba, worked in maintenance on day shift, and before long, got wind of one of these episodes from the ongoing soap opera. He came to the plant one night with a Louisville Slugger branded with ole' Joe's name all over the barrel. Fortunately, I caught wind of this before Bubba made it very far into the plant, and I got the police involved before it got out of hand. Unfortunately, this created quite a distraction from the work needed on our shift, and productivity suffered. In retrospect, I should have stepped into the situation sooner and spoken to Joe and Betty about their soap opera and its impact on the plant. This was a great lesson for me. Had the police not gotten to Bubba when they did, he would have whacked ole' Joe over the left field silo, and I might have been the next one on deck!

Work Hours

It's very easy to say that the factory will work the hours needed to accomplish the job. It is also very easy to assume that if overtime work hours are scheduled, people will show up to do it. Don't believe it. There are some plant cultures in which overtime is actively sought by employees and readily accepted. There are others in which overtime is loathed and actively avoided. These are not regional differences; they are a function of plant culture and "usual and customary" practices. In the former case, you will have serious problems if you do not schedule overtime equitably. People will fight over the extra hours. In the latter, you will have serious problems if you don't schedule overtime by first asking for volunteers.

Of course, if you are supervising in a union plant, then the rules are set by contract, and you won't have much leeway. If you do not have a union plant, the odds are that overtime guidelines are outlined by your employee handbook, and you will have discretion. Use it wisely.

Racial, Religious, and Sexual Differences

We will touch on this only briefly as most situations are ruled by law, and we don't pretend to be lawyers. This is one area in which you must consult your corporate personnel department for guidance.

To a great extent, most companies guide their supervision and management very strictly in areas of potential discrimination. These guidelines are usually well thought out and address legally mandated requirements. But like all guidelines, they cannot be all-encompassing. Common sense, being the least common of the senses, should not be relied on here. It may be common sense that Bill can better lift that 75 lb. bag than Sally, but Bill may well resent lifting all the 75 lb. bags while Sally does inventory. Also, Sally might resent your assumption that Bill should do the lifting. One common statement that we have encouraged to various, management teams goes something like this: "We do not have men jobs; we do not have women jobs; we have jobs."

All in all it comes down to this: know your culture, know your people, and understand what is and isn't acceptable to them. In no circumstance should you let these cultural issues lead you to break company policies or the law, and sometimes you will have to enforce a little culture shock for the overall good of the plant. More on this a bit later.

Union and Non-Union

What are the differences between managing in Union-free plants and Union plants? Our answer may surprise you -not much.

Carl-

My first job out of college was in a Union factory in Seattle, WA. The union was the United Brick and Clay Workers, since folded several times into the United Steelworkers. Frankly, half the time I didn't even know it was a union plant because the Plant Manager, Big Mike Kochanek, made sure the union was irrelevant in the daily lives of the employees. The factory was well-run and profitable, and I was blessed that Big Mike was my first boss.

The second company I worked for as plant manager was a union free plant in Cleveland, Mississippi. The plant had never been well-run, was in disarray, and cost me the longest 18 months I'd ever lived. I exercised my development plan out of the organization as quickly as practical.

Now wait a minute ... we just wrote that there isn't much difference between union-free and union plants, and then went on to illustrate huge differences between the two. What gives? The difference in the operations was not union status. The difference was leadership and culture.

Carl - Big Mike had been a very tough but fair boss and took a particular interest in my development. He told me something I was to never forget:"If you manage a union-free plant then run it like a union plant."

Huh?

What does a union contract offer employees? Recognized work rules, consistency, and fair treatment. What does a well-run union free plant offer employees? Recognized work rules, consistency, and fair treatment. In the former case, employees pay a union to bargain as a unit for these conditions. In the latter case, the employees get it for free in the form of a well-written, employee handbook. The only difference between the two is that if you, as a supervisor or manager ignore your contract, you will be formally grieved; and if you ignore your well-written, employee handbook, you will pay a far higher price in the disaffection of your employees. The grievance is preferable as it will be resolved in favor of one party or another, and everyone goes their merry way. Disaffected employees who know you could have ruled in their favor, but didn't, stay disaffected for a long time if they believe you ruled capriciously.

So now you may wonder if it is not better for a supervisor or manager to work in a union plant. It is, but only if you don't care about the long term future of the plant. The restrictions that come with a union contract on work rules, conflict resolution, and plant creativity make the union-free environment much more desirable -if you do care about the long term future. Of course, if you don't care, you probably won't read this book, and the need to convince you doesn't exist; but if you do care, run your operation according to your well-written handbook and follow it like a union/management contract. If the handbook isn't well-written, get it changed. Also, you don't have to wait until contract negotiations to do it. Recognize that if you are running a union-free plant, and an organization effort is started; and your people grant authority to a bargaining unit, then you will get a union. You will get the one you deserve.

We have looked at culture from the aspects of regionalism, nepotism, work hours, and union vs. union-free. These are elements of the plant culture but not the foundation. Let's look at a couple of different meanings for the word culture:

- *The quality in a person or society that arises from a concern for what is regarded as excellence.*
- *Development of improvement of the mind through training or education.*

Notice the key words in the definitions - *excellence* and *improvement*. Developing a unique culture for the plant that sets high expectations for performance, quality, engagement, compassion, and respect should be your ultimate goal as a leader. For us, the understanding of the importance of plant culture became the true foundation.

One conversation that we find ourselves giving to others more and more involves *respect* to each member of the plant family. We often say that the operator cleaning the pits out has just as vital a role as the President of the company. If this operator does not complete the task at hand in a timely, accurate, and safe manner, the plant will suffer. The only difference between a President and an operator is that more people can be operators than can be presidents. Show respect to all on your team, learn their names, be *On The Plant Floor* daily at multiple times, and realize that *you* must earn their respect. Teach your management team that *respect* is the cornerstone.

Bryan-

I started my career in a plant as a production operator learning the ropes of manufacturing. I worked in production on different shifts for 3 years and transferred to lab technician. This actually paid less than my production job. However, it allowed me to be in several sequences within the plant learning a great deal about the entire, manufacturing process. After working in the lab for another 5 years, I was promoted to supervisor.

My dad worked in manufacturing at an aluminum, processing plant for 47 years and ran a complex machine for over 25 years of his career. This equipment split large rolls of aluminum into foil that was only .002"thick. This thin foil was used in chewing gum wrappers. Dad always worked in production and turned down all opportunities for promotion. He was not anti-management, but he preferred to have more control of his time on and off the clock.

When I first told Dad that I had taken a supervisory position, he gave me some advice."Ok son, so now you think you are going to be a big shot in a management position? Just remember what I am telling you, and you will do well. The same hands and fingers that you may step on climbing the corporate ladder are attached to the same behind you will have to kiss on your way back down."At the time, I did not appreciate his words as much as I do now. (It was all about showing the respect and compassion to everyone involved.) Without fail, it is the same speech I have given to each first time supervisor that I have been associated with or have promoted.

My oldest brother, who had worked his way into management years before I did, was also very helpful in making sure I got off to a good start. After my first 6 months as a new supervisor, I learned that my failed approach of"I'm the boss. Do what I say, or I will fire you,"and my attitude of thinking operators"must just be too dumb to learn the equipment," and that maintenance is just"too sorry to fix anything,"needed to take a new direction. My brother offered the following advice:"You only need to learn two methods for successful management: when to buy a pizza and when to give a foot in the butt." For years this did not really make sense to me and just seemed so old school. But as time passed, it became relevant and important to the way I managed on the job. It represents the understanding of when it is best to reward and best to correct. If you do either at the wrong time, it can be detrimental; and you will lose ground in developing the plant culture.

For example, if you have an operator that is struggling, and you recognize they are having some problems off the field as well as on the field, is it really the best time to ride them hard and lower the boom? If their problems off the field are much more serious to them than their work performance, probably not. Understanding they could use some personal encouragement along with more specific work direction, might just do the trick. Incidentally, if you are not firm and consistent with performance expectations, you lose forward momentum. Setting the bar higher and higher is a must in each plant and each sequence.

So how do you know when to reward and when to correct? It takes time, experience (asking others that have both), and most of all, PAYING ATTENTION. Be engaged, focused, driven; do not be a casual member of the plant management team. You did not sign up to be casual. You signed up to lead. Leaders are committed to the overall good of the plant. Know your people, know your operation, and lead them to form a great culture on the plant floor.

In summary, recognize the culture of the area and develop a plant culture that promotes excellence. It will serve you well at all levels within the plant, the local community, and corporate. It will also represent the company as a whole very well. Remember the key terms that you will see repeatedly in this work that have helped form positive and rewarding cultures down through our years: respect, engagement, disclosure, integrity, compassion, and humility.

17

Celebrating Victories Large and Small

This time it ain't about you

Nope, it ain't about you or anybody else in management. This time it's about the folks – the ones who make your factory go. In a previous chapter, we showed you that not everyone is like you. In this chapter, we will show you that despite their individuality, most all of 'em will like celebrations and recognition; there is an effective way and a useless way to "party on." We will also show you why it is important to party on.

Virtually all companies go to some effort to give a bonus, however small, to the troops at Christmas time. These are corporate devices and the only thing you have to do to get your turkey or gift certificate is to be an employee. This is not a celebration of victory (unless you are celebrating simply staying in business for another year), it is a *bonus*. And that's cool, really. We believe that the holiday season is a perfect time for passing out bonuses to everyone. Most people appreciate the bonus, even you, but it doesn't come from you. It comes from your handy-dandy corporate office, and your only involvement is to have your personnel guy distribute the envelopes. Not really what you would call coming from the heart, now is it, or a great way to engage with the folks that really do all the work? No, we are talking about celebrating achievement by individuals, teams, and the entire plant. These achievements can happen any day of the year, not just at the holidays.

Bad Ways to Recognize Achievements

Man, we have seen plenty of bad ways for factory management to celebrate good performance. Here are just a few:

- Employee of the Month: So, you have a factory with say, 200 hourly employees and 25 salaried, non-exempt folks, and you have one "Employee of the Month"? Aarrgghhh! You might as well pass out 224 notes that say "you suck!" Recognizing *one* employee benefits *one* person. In effect, you are saying that 224 people made no contribution to your factory. You know that isn't true unless you have a really bad culture.

- One month of preferred parking: See Employee of the Month. We have seen the Employee of the Month parking space perpetually vacant after it became known as the "my car gets keyed" parking space.

- Committee Awards: We inflicted this one upon ourselves. We had what we thought was a great idea. It was decided to have people nominate outstanding employees from the plant floor and have a committee determine the winners, and we avoided the Employee of the Month problem with multiple awards. The committee consisted of the plant manager, assistant plant manager, maintenance manager, a supervisor or two, and the plant personnel manager. There were cool prizes, and we started off very pleased with ourselves. The whole thing lasted about 3 months and crashed with a resounding thud. There weren't many nominations, and it seemed that the few we had were the same, three people every month. The committee meetings were also painfully long and involved. We remembered one key principle to recognizing people: don't make *them* determine who should be recognized. Do it yourself, and leave the committees for something else.

- The catalogue: These awards, unfortunately, are very popular in the corporate world. At least they are popular with some managers because they don't have to do anything; some catalogue company does all the work. That is also some catalogue company that never met a single employee who works with you. Most commonly, the catalogue awards are used to recognize length of service. You have a catalogue with clocks, money clips, watches, and other impersonal "gifts," and the employee gets to pick out what they want – the longer the service, the bigger the gift. Maybe somebody out there wants a catalogue company to mail an employee (some weeks later) a mantle clock for thirty years of service. Us? We would prefer to hand the employee an engraved watch as the rest of the plant looks on. Be personal, be real.

Any reward or recognition that removes you, the manager, from the process is bad. Yes, you are busy, but is there anything more important than your people? We think not. We hope you aren't, but you might be asking right now, "Why do I need to recognize and reward people?" If you are new to management, we will forgive you the question and provide the answer. It's about motivation. Motivated people are odds on to excel. They contribute to the bottom line over and above their salary. They are happy and are a joy to lead. Motivated people also make your life easier, so let's go motivate 'em! Hold on there just a minute, cowboy, you can't do it. Huh? You say, "What about all those books about motivating people I've been reading?" We say - throw those books away. YOU cannot motivate people. People can motivate only themselves. Your job, Mr. Manager, is to build a culture in which people are more likely to be self-motivated.

"All motivation is self-motivation. Your family, your boss, or your co-workers can try to get your engine going, but until you decide what to accomplish, nothing will happen."
—Seth Godin

So while you can't motivate people, you surely as a manager can *de-motivate* them. Celebrating victories large and small is part of the culture which encourages self-motivation; not celebrating them (or doing it badly) will de-motivate your people. Count on it.

Large Victories

Usually, but not always, large victories are group efforts. Examples of group, large victories are exceeding monthly performance indicators, no lost-time accidents, successful start-ups, and expansion commissioning. Group, large victories should always be celebrated with the full group. Individual, large victories may be long-term service anniversaries or promotion to a higher level. Depending on the culture and the people, these victories may be private with just you and the employee or may be better in a larger, group setting. Your determination of what constitutes a large victory is just that - yours. You know what is best for your operation, and if you are guided by celebrating large victories when targets are exceeded or significant events occur, you will be on the right track.

Our experience has shown us that virtually everyone likes two things: food and company-logoed clothing. That's right, barbecue and tee-shirts. These two awards form the basis for an easy to manage celebration process. In the case of safety awards, we had a simple program. If the plant has no lost-time accidents in a calendar quarter, everybody eats. The supervisors and managers did all the cooking (tenderized steaks on a hoagie roll and potato chips), serving and clean-up. The menu was less important than the fact that the hourly employees were waited on by their bosses. We expanded the lunch hour from 30 minutes to one hour, so everyone could be served. Tailor the menu to your regional preferences, and keep it simple. If your experience is like ours, you will find that people will begin asking to bring in covered dishes to add to the menu. By all means, allow them to do so. Before long, your modest investment in steaks and potato chips will turn into a feast as people bring in baked beans, potato salad, and desserts. *(We sure do love fried pies!)*

So in one very simple and inexpensive program, you have allowed your employees to motivate themselves to be safer. Win-win: *(Carl-I can already hear your corporate safety department worrying about people hiding accidents so they can get a free steak lunch. That's a concern, and one you handle by stressing to your people that any action like that will kill the program forever. And in over 35 years of cooking for employees, I never, ever saw anybody conceal an accident for a lunch. Besides, most employee handbooks clearly state that concealing accidents will lead to termination.)*

If cooking for your employees is impractical, you can have a lunch catered in. This isn't as much fun and should only be done if there is no alternative. We have seen places in which there is no suitable area for cooking. Arranging for a place to cook in the future would be a worthy project.

These days of celebrations might be long ones for the plant manager because all shifts must be served. We've cooked steaks at 3:00 am, but we never minded it. Leaving out your employees simply because they aren't on day shift, just ain't right. The only reason to leave people out is if they are on vacation or absent. If you have a weekend shift, you are going have to figure out a way for them to get fed as well. Whatever you do, treat all the employees equally.

Smaller groups call for a different reward method. Let's say you have a new machine installed in record time by the sequence operators and maintenance group. This achievement may not warrant plant celebration, but you want to recognize the group. In this case, food is not a real good idea. One part of the plant celebrating with a meal doesn't always sit well with the rest of the plant. Instead, award them with company-logoed clothing. Satin, baseball jackets embroidered with the employee's name and position are perfect for events like this. You will be amazed how often you will see these recognition jackets worn in the plant and outside in the community.

Follow one simple rule with clothing. Big achievement = Big reward. Tee shirts and caps should be awarded often and to many. Down-filled winter coats should be offered rarely and only to a few with justified accomplishments.

Small Victories

Small victories are most often individual or won by a sequence. We prize cleanliness and order, and sequences that either complete a successful cleanup or maintain extraordinary standards should be recognized by the supervisor and manager. There are a hundred other things you might feel are worth recognition as well. This is just one example. Clothing works great here. Tee-shirts, polo shirts, caps, backpacks all with company logos are appropriate here. Individual accomplishments such as productivity improvement suggestions or an operator breaking a single machine production record can be recognized. Do this also with clothing, or the plant manager should make his way down to the machine and shake the operator's hand. Congratulation should be given with a promise to tell the vice-president about the record. You can tailor your recognition methods to your plant culture, but the important thing is that you do it.

The Personal

You may have a lot of people working for you and may not know each and every person's individual life, but you have a personnel supervisor/manager, and you should enlist them to aid in recognizing personal achievements or milestones. They can monthly prepare birthday cards for you to sign and personalize for your employees. The 30 minutes a month you spend wishing an employee a happy birthday will yield happy dividends for you and the employee.

Your personnel supervisor can keep you informed of family births and graduations, so that you can wish the employee congratulations. There will also be unhappy moments in a person's life where you can offer condolences. As always, remember that people do have lives outside the factory and are human beings, not resources. (*Carl —Yet again, I say I loathe the term human "resources".*) Of course, it's even better if you know your people well enough that you don't need help with the personal acknowledgements of the events in people's lives, and some of you may be good enough to do it on your own without help. That's wonderful and a goal worthy of achieving.

Recognize victories both large and small and do it personally. The money and effort invested in celebration will be returned to you many times over. You will find that some of the happiest moments in your career will come at 3:00 am over a charcoal grill while barbecuing steaks for your employees. This may appear to be a simple and basic thing to do in today's factory, but it's a large part of forming the culture needed for continued success.

18

Spreading The Pain

Entitlements & Improvements
Beyond Scratching The Surface

The Well-Run Plant

When you walk into a manufacturing plant for the first time what do you look for to determine if the plant is managed well and has effective leadership? First impressions as well as follow-up impressions can say much about your engagement and pride of the institution. Having production problems, equipment issues, customer complaints, or cost concerns are enough to guarantee that you get plenty of unwanted attention. Add to these frustrations that you are constantly getting drilled over housekeeping and organization, and pretty soon, you reach the nearest exit door.

The well led plant is a quiet place. Even those who enter your facility and do not have any knowledge of the production process or any manufacturing experience will detect this. We know too well the chaos that can be involved on the plant floor. Equipment is down, personnel are scrambling, and there appears to be no sense to the madness. A factory that is full of drama and allows this chaos to unfold before a visitor's eye will indicate a poor managed plant without the needed culture. A well-run plant may seem dull as everything flows seemingly like a fine-tuned engine. The drama has been replaced by developing a culture that anticipates crises and converts them into routine.

Here are some points that will ensure that you and your team make good, first impressions as well as substantial lasting impressions:

- Housekeeping (critical to enforce into the culture as routine)

- Organization (everything has a place, stacked straight, leveled, and squared)

- Equipment is maintained and kept in "looks new" condition. Wipe down, paint, and do not permit the cabinets or panels to be cluttered with items that do not belong there. Your operator or other staff may not be able to learn all the intrinsic details to maximize the equipment's performance, but they very well can keep it clean and organized.

- Management offices: if desks are covered, the floors are a mess, and the place is basically a pigsty, it is a flawed culture.

- Restrooms: the condition of your plant's bathrooms is an area that you should be proud of and not ashamed for visitors to utilize. (People notice this area as much as any.)

- Dress: being on the plant floor is a dirty job in most operations. However, requiring your management team to look professional is a must. Anyone should be able to spot a manager on the plant floor and distinguish them from the rest of the workers. A shirt with a collar and Docker style pants will suffice. Anything beyond this, and you might be afraid to get down and get dirty – that ain't the culture needed.

Do not confuse motion with progress. A rocking horse keeps moving but does not make any progress. — Alfred A. Montapert

Alfred Armand Montapert wrote the book "The Supreme Philosophy of Man: The Laws of Life." It is an amazing book written in 1970 that is both practical and realistic. Mr. Montapert discusses 47 fundamental laws of life that all of us can learn from to maximize our full potential regardless of race, gender, geographic location, or profession. Here are a few more quotes from the book that we have found most helpful.

- *"The greatest things are accomplished by individual people, not by committees or companies."*

- *"To accomplish great things we must first dream, then visualize the plan — act- and believe."*

- *"In Texas, years ago, almost all the oil came from surface operations. Then someone got the idea that there was a greater source of supply down deeper. A well was drilled 5000 ft deep. The result? A gusher. Too many of us operate on the surface. We never go deep enough to find supernatural resources. The result is, we never operate at our best. More time and investment is involved to go deep but a gusher will pay off."*

In this chapter, we are going to go well beyond the surface and equip you with tools that allow you to dig much deeper into process improvement. You have already heard us mention that we grew to remove the term "departments" and replace it with "sequences." Departments can signal a division of groups that builds walls and does not interact with other areas as needed. While one "department" may be performing magnificently, the department before them or after them is struggling. In unison with the plant culture, here again, the whole will be greater than the sum of its parts. The flow in the plant is hindered when certain areas are building empires and others are falling. "Department" can create independence rather than unity. Using the term "sequence" creates a known belief that each area is only a part of the whole. Think of sequence as a chain on a motor. If one link in the chain breaks, the motor stops as well as production. Sequence A provides a service to sequence B and sequence B to sequence C and so on. If any sequence breaks down or has quality defects, it directly impacts the other sequences and the process as a whole.

Improving The Sequence

Process improvements are an obvious constant need on the plant floor. The competition today is greater than ever both domestically and foreign. Technology advancements have turned today's manufacturing environment into a lean, mean, fighting machine. Regardless of the technology with a superb controls system, the more the equipment, the more maintenance and training are required. Today's process improvement is littered with terms such as lean manufacturing, Six Sigma, and the Toyota production system. We are going to give you two realistic terms that drive all process improvements: *Commitment and Compassion.*

Commitment is an agreement or pledge to do something in the future. *Compassion* is to suffer with. Do not sit around waiting on emotions to drive your improvements. Do it out of obedience. Do something now. Your commitment cannot merely be words stated in group meetings to encourage others to "do more." The proof is in the pudding, so to speak, so here is where your ability to lead or falter will be most apparent. Can you take the plant or your sequence to the next level? Will you only maintain the status quo, or are you willing to rock the boat? Your individual investment of energy, skill, ability, and eagerness will be evident in the work performed. To better understand a sequence's struggles, you need to feel their pain. Staying on the plant floor constantly with a sequence that is plagued with issues will undoubtedly put to rest many of your presumptuous considerations from afar, such as, there must be a magic wand or secret button that no one can find. Go get the facts and lead the team's effort to higher ground.

Process Reliability

Total Plant Process Reliability

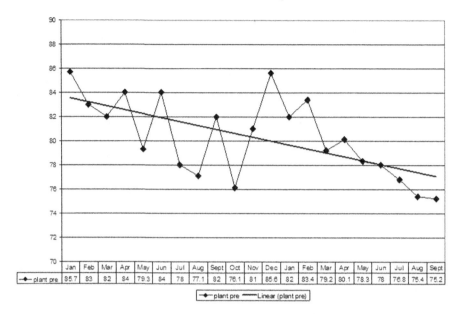

	Jan	Feb	Mar	Apr	May	Jun	Jul	Aug	Sept	Oct	Nov	Dec	Jan	Feb	Mar	Apr	May	Jun	Jul	Aug	Sept
plant pre	85.7	83	82	84	79.3	84	78	77.1	82	76.1	81	85.6	82	83.4	79.2	80.1	78.3	78	76.8	75.4	75.2

plant pre — Linear (plant pre)

That's an ugly looking situation and a true one that we faced not long ago with an aging operation. Process reliability (PRE) is a tool we implemented to gather the data needed to better determine the dependability of our plant sequences. PRE takes into consideration many elements of noise that can obscure the actual effectiveness of an area. Scheduled downtime obviously is planned and does not impact the productivity of a sequence near as much as unscheduled downtime. Change-overs are also another element that can mask the true effectiveness of a sequence. If one sequence runs more SKUs than another, the time required for die changes, color changes, line changes, etc. must be considered as part of the equation. Notice how the chart above is all over the place with no rhyme or reason but certainly trending the wrong direction. This chart is the PLANT total of several sequences within that are killing the productivity. Guess what matches the trend of productivity going south?

Plant Unit Cost

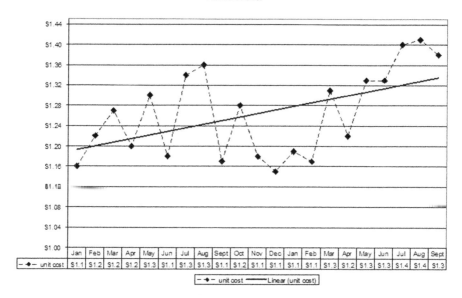

	Jan	Feb	Mar	Apr	May	Jun	Jul	Aug	Sept	Oct	Nov	Dec	Jan	Feb	Mar	Apr	May	Jun	Jul	Aug	Sept
unit cost	$1.1	$1.2	$1.2	$1.2	$1.3	$1.1	$1.3	$1.3	$1.1	$1.2	$1.1	$1.1	$1.1	$1.1	$1.3	$1.2	$1.3	$1.3	$1.4	$1.4	$1.3

unit cost ———Linear (unit cost)

You got it, unit cost is all over the place also and certainly headed north in the wrong direction. This was a bleak situation that needed a quick turnaround, or the plant faced consolidation into another division. You can see within both of these charts that there are splashes of brilliance and moments of victory. But stability and dependability are lacking and that makes forecasting a nightmare. Notice that both charts cover a 2 yr long process and that all the bad did not happen over night.

Total Plant Process Reliability

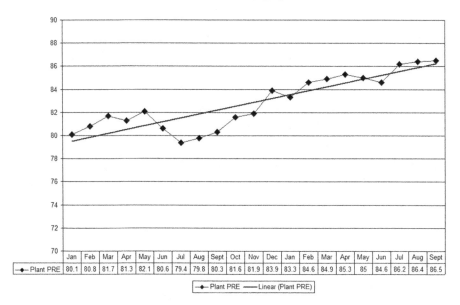

	Jan	Feb	Mar	Apr	May	Jun	Jul	Aug	Sept	Oct	Nov	Dec	Jan	Feb	Mar	Apr	May	Jun	Jul	Aug	Sept
Plant PRE	80.1	80.8	81.7	81.3	82.1	80.6	79.4	79.8	80.3	81.6	81.9	83.9	83.3	84.6	84.9	85.3	85	84.6	86.2	86.4	86.5

Plant PRE —— Linear (Plant PRE)

Now there's a much better actual chart showing stability and steady improvement. Again, notice that this productivity chart covers a 2 yr period also, and that all the good things did not happen over night. In case you are wondering, yes, the unit cost went south as the productivity went north. What did it take to make this happen? It for sure was no magic wand!

Entitlements

What are entitlements, and what the heck does this have to do with the plant floor? Well, we are certainly not referring to your typical thoughts that involve the guarantee of benefits such as Social Security or Medicare. *(At least all of us but Carl aren't — Bryan)* Entitlement is the "best" that the line could theoretically achieve if it were running at 100% uptime, that is, with no unplanned downtime, scrap, rework, and running the designated rate of production. 100% uptime could also be referred to as OEE (Overall Equipment Effectiveness). One of the roles of a Six Sigma professional is to quantify the process performance (Short Term and Long Term capability), and based on the true process entitlement and process shift, establish the right strategy to reach the established, performance objective. While we are students and trainers of Six Sigma, there are tons of works that will do this subject more justice. Our ability to establish entitlements involved creating opportunities and accountabilities for our team. A direct engagement with the troops ensures that sequences and individuals that are successful work with other sequences and individuals that are struggling. *Spreading The Pain* is all about developing groups of individuals to work through process improvements. A measurement system such as PRE must be put in place to capture, monitor, and evaluate the needed data. Regardless of how bad, an initial baseline should be established to determine the metrics needed to develop realistic goals of where you want to be. Below is an example of an entitlement tracking that involved scheduled downtime for one sequence.

WEEKLY MONITORING							
SEQUENCE A	Hours	New	Results				
	per	Target	Week				Responsibility
Scheduled	Week		8-Aug	15-Aug	22-Aug	29-Aug	
Rinses	3.29	2.96	4.04	3.25	4.09	4.59	Jones
Glaze Color Change	2.65	2.39	4.85	2.50	4.77	4.50	Smith
Die Change	2.78	1.01	2.90	3.50	4.30	1.37	Lewis
Clay Color Change	1.17	0.94	0.50	2.00	0.00	0.00	Williams
Out of Cars	1.64	0.00	0.00	0.00	0.00	0.00	ALL SEQUENCE SUPERVISORS
Total these categories	11.53	7.29	12.29	11.25	13.16	10.46	
Total All Scheduled	38.1		26.00	28.08	48.24	28.19	

What is being tracked in the above table includes the hours of unscheduled downtime per week, various categories of the sequence involved, and those responsible for the tracking and improvements. Now let's take a look at unscheduled downtime in the same sequence.

Unscheduled	Hours per Week	New Target	WEEKLY MONITORING Results Week				Responsibility
			8-Aug	15-Aug	22-Aug	29-Aug	
	2d 1/4						
Destackers	1.66	1.58	1.14	0.82	0.80	0.91	Geary / Lewis
Takeout Head	2.46	2.34	2.89	2.85	4.80	3.03	Sorrell / Smith
Fettling Table	2.24	2.13	2.28	3.99	2.25	4.16	Ray
Transfer Head	1.61	1.35	2.54	9.03	13.98	6.02	Williams
Hapman	2.38	1.00	3.98	4.22	0.65	1.60	Smith / Baker
Wide Belt	3.78	3.60	2.56	4.18	6.80	4.00	Geary / Jones
Die Wash	3.33	2.22	1.23	2.40	0.90	1.17	Smith / Lewis
Charger	4.78	2.00	6.05	4.08	1.31	2.77	Williams / Sorrell
Pawls/Platens	1.57	1.29	1.48	5.23	3.82	0.70	Allen
Fired Hooks	1.15	0.86	0.79	1.26	0.81	1.36	Allen
Tote Box Heads	1.12	0.96	1.10	1.35	1.65	2.79	Jones / Smith / Lewis
Press Mechanical	2.13	1.70	0.69	1.26	7.11	1.89	Ray / Baker
Fired Chain Table	0.65	0.62	3.15	1.28	0.32	0.97	Baker
Press Electrical	5.40	1.85	6.53	5.01	8.54	4.09	Ray
Total These Categories	34.26	23.49	36.41	46.96	53.74	35.46	
Total All Unscheduled			71.24	70.65	76.66	61.39	
Total All Entitlement DT	45.8	30.79	48.70	58.21	66.90	45.92	
Total All Downtime	91.8		97.2	98.7	104.9	89.6	

The same type of data is gathered allowing those responsible for tracking status and improvements to develop action items. Without forcing the foundation of data gathering, you are like a blind squirrel that only finds a nut every once in a while.

The sequence teams were always a diverse group. They were critical to success, allowing those responsible to be engaged with the talent needed. Maintenance and electrical associates are part of the accountability to ensure improvements gain maximum, forward momentum. Engineering is also involved as well as bringing in outside support and specialists. Meetings are scheduled each week for multiple sequences. This allows cross-team collaboration for those making progress and those needing more assistance. All of the individuals are responsible for tracking their data, creating charts, and driving the improvements. The top leadership of the plant monitors the master file of all the sequences while engaging in the meetings to provide support, capital, and barrier removal as needed. Do not permit blame to cast shadows on improvement efforts. The assertion that "somebody else will not let me do anything" should always be suspected as a cover-up. As you will notice, the authors' names are listed under some of the responsible areas as we shared the pain in order to share the glory we worked so diligently to find.

One of the things that quickly emerged from tracking the data and making changes for improvement was the need to upgrade our PM program. Preventive and predicted maintenance can become cool buzz words in manufacturing with huge sources of cost. Somewhere between running equipment until it fails and changing out parts is the history to determine the actual need. This entitlement program will help gather the history that production and maintenance need to make the best decisions. Checklists for operators and maintenance became the norm in the operation. We reviewed these checklists with operators, supervisors, and maintenance so that all had a voice in the process. Below is an example of the operator checklist.

PM Checklist for Green Loader - Operator

Item	Frequency	Look for	Responsible Party	PM	Notify
Check cups	shift	torn, missing or loose cups	operator	replace as needed	Supervisor
Positive stops	shift	cracked tile chipped tile	operator	adjust as needed	Supervisor
Check foam on Heads	shift	torn or missing foam	operator	replace as needed	Supervisor
Gates	shift	loose, cracking tile	operator	adjust as needed	Mechanic
Guillotine	shift	loose, cracking tile	operator	adjust as needed	Mechanic

Long term solutions: Standardize cups to all green and yellow cups on all heads....done.
Standardize positive stops plates on all heads to the same style.

This type of checklist improves the operator's skills on the job and allows them to evolve in order to become experts of their equipment. Proper safety is a must, so training is required before this can be implemented. Here is another example of a checklist that is performed by maintenance.

PM Checklist for Pawls/Platens - Mechanic				
Item	Frequency	Responsible Party	PM	Notify
Rack/Gears	monthly	Mechanic	every six months	Supervisor
Actuator	weekly	Mechanic	every 3 months	Supervisor
Lift cylinder Leaks, loose	monthly	Mechanic	every 3 months	Supervisor
Platens Warped/loose	monthly	Mechanic	every 6 months	Supervisor
Pullbacks cylinders/loose	monthly	Mechanic	every 3 months	Supervisor
Long Term solution - replace drive for setter chain on 310 line with servo motor				

We have found that grouping the responsibility of PMs, checklists, and maintenance needs with the sequence supervisor and maintenance manager creates the best chance for success. Of course, conflicts will occur that require leadership to maintain progress, but this is part of the process of getting a sequence to the next level.

Process Experts

Unless you are in a mega-plant with tons of resources, including multiple staffs of engineering from industrial to electrical to mechanical, you will need the plant to have internal, process experts at the level of supervisors and operators. During the entitlement process, your team will begin to recognize the mysteries of why some lines (identical to others) run better or worse. Most often this will require careful benchmarking of the lines involved. Time studies of each step within the line can be a critical tool to figure out the anomalies. Below is an example of a sequence that had 4 identical lines, but none of them performed the same.

Line Speeds

Seconds timed	Line 1	Line 2	Line 3	Line 4
Total cycle time	8.5	8.8	8.5	8.7
Oven belt raise/lower time	1.1	1.0	1.0	1.0
Rotator Pause	0.1	0.3	0.1	0.1
Rotator Spin	1.2	1.2	1.2	1.2
Board Tilt	2.9	2.8	2.1	2.9
Board Raise/Lower	2.8	2.8	2.8	2.8
Speed-up belt	7.0	7.0	7.0	7.0
Take-A-Way chain	7.2	7.7	7.3	8.0
Crossover #1	9.2	9.7	9.2	9.5
Separator Belt	3.0	3.1	3.1	3.1
Main chain ON	4.3	4.1	4.1	4.0
Main chain OFF	4.0	4.0	4.9	4.5
Crossover #2	3.0/3.0	3.0/3.0	3.0/3.0	3.1/3.1
Board Loader Back/Forward	1.7/1.7	1.6/1.8	1.7/1.7	2.0/2.0
Board Loader Up/Down	0.8	0.6	1.0	1.3
Select Heads	A	B	C	D
Up/Down	0.65	0.52	0.74	0.9
To Tile (Empty)	0.32	0.3	0.87	0.12
(With) product	0.54	0.67	0.98	0.32

Notice the variation in the times between the lines performing the same function. A deeper dive indicates that the lines are not identical. What we found were small motor size differences, sprocket changes that were incorrect, and PLC timers that were adjusted differently. As we began to standardize the lines, more and more operators struggled less when they rotated from machine to machine. Also, this allowed us to zero in on the key areas of the line that we could tweak and push for increased output and more consistent production. Details, details, and more details are required to get to the root cause of a real issue. This is why you choose to monitor every single step of the line- to ensure that nothing is overlooked or that assumptions are proved. The downtime sheets need to include detailed comments and specifics of the occurrence. For example, a belt breaks on the rotator head on line 3, and you have 45 minutes of unscheduled downtime. This event should be detailed with more specifics, such as:

THE 2ND BELT ON THE NORTH PULLEY OF THE EAST MOTOR BROKE. THE BELT DID NOT LOOK WORN AND OUR NOTES SHOW THAT IT BROKE LAST WEEK ALSO. This level of specifics of occurrence will challenge you to find the root cause which must not be the belt in this case. Looking at more historical data, you realize that this is the 4th belt in 4 weeks on the same motor and pulley that has been changed. You and your mechanic now start digging for the core issue and discover that the pulley has a bad bearing. It's a decent-size job to change the bearing, but you bite the bullet and do it on your shift. Your mechanic has to stay over an hour to complete and gets assistance from the next shift's mechanic. Ironically enough, the next shift mechanic admits that he has been greasing the bearing every night to get through the shift because of the downtime required to fix correctly.

This is fundamentally wrong, but we all know it's a reality on the plant floor. We are not condoning this at all. In fact, it's a management problem and not a maintenance problem. Somehow, the culture creates a fear to do the right thing through poor leadership that did not define the expectations clearly. If your plant or sequence is struggling and plagued with multiple failures, the new culture that you institute may in fact, get worse before it gets better at the onset. Make sure to inform those upstream that your turnaround effort will need their support and understanding in order to be successful. Initially, downtime and production cost may increase because of the time required to get the lines in shape. Upstream may only want to believe that you have the magic wand, and if so... you are in for a real bumpy ride. However, commit to the cause with fortitude and march on with determination to see it through to success.

Below is a chart that we are still very proud of to this day. One of the sequence supervisors truly fought the need for the entitlement program. We fought harder and drew the line in the sand that basically said, "Get with the program, or be prepared to get out of the way." You know, "get on the bus, or the bus will run you over." In just a few months, we began to make a few changes on one of the four lines within the sequence, and it started to rise out of the ashes. The sequence supervisor became the process expert that quickly took charge of the improvements. As mentioned, it took details, and details, and more details to uncover the root causes of some of the problems as well as how to maximize the lines. We got the process started, but the sequence supervisor was soon driving the bus, and we got out of the way.

Sequence B Productivity

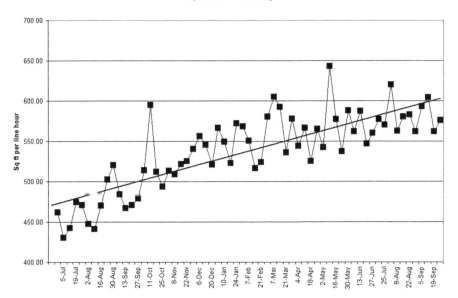

Now we all know too well that you can make a chart say whatever you want to, but eventually, the numbers must match the actuals, or it becomes obvious to all involved upstream and downstream. Plus, the integrity of the plant rides on the key leadership to enforce full and true disclosure. The weekly entitlement meetings are essential to not only monitor progress, but to also create action items. Action items are not necessarily commitments. They are intentions, and intentions will change over time. Do not let action items put you in a straight jacket. Instead, appreciate as the sequence supervisor or responsible person for the entitlement, that you are charged with putting together the resources needed to drive the improvement efforts.

Spreading the pain will encourage sequences to share information and process improvement techniques throughout the plant. The supervisor of Sequence B (the great productivity chart above) soon became involved with other sequences to champion their efforts as well. Do not underestimate the power of persistence and positive competition in the plant. It encourages others to excel by empowering them as well as holding them accountable for all areas of their sequence. At the plant manager level, ask some basic questions repeatedly and follow these guidelines to be most effective:

- "What needs to be done?"

- "What is right for the plant?" Focus on what is right instead of who is right.

- Help develop the action plans.

- Take responsibility for decisions.

- Take responsibility for communicating.

- Focus on the opportunities more than the problems.

- Run productive meetings / keeping them concise and infrequent.

- Focus on strengths more than weaknesses. Ask "what can a man do" instead of listing all the things "he cannot do."

- Say "we" much more than "I".

Spreading The Pain through entitlements to gain maximum process improvement may not be the most popular avenue to take. However, having certain groups that excel while others fail is not spreading the talent and knowledge to promote full plant recovery.

19

Disaster Strikes

We could offer countless experiences that might be labeled as disasters both personally and professionally. However, recalling the event below makes most others appear trivial.

Bryan –

It was Sunday night around 10:00 pm on May 4, 2003. I was at the plant with my right hand man, Mitch, working on various color work, matching samples for the following week. We had several storms during the week, and it was unusually hot for the month of May. Around 10:30 pm, storm sirens started going off around the city of Jackson, TN, and the siren at the plant sounded. I pulled the plant shift supervisor aside and told him to shut down the lines and get everyone to the designated storm shelters; which, in our case, were the concrete reinforced restrooms. *(Do you have an evacuation or emergency plan???)*

Mitch and I both lived on the south side of town and wanted desperately to get home to our families. Sunday night was not our normal work schedule, but often we spent time on weekends, nights, holidays, etc … you know, whatever it took to meet the production orders. We both headed outside around 10:40 pm, and the sky was an unusual yellowish, gray color that I had not seen before. I hope not to see this again. We wished each other the best and hit the road with full steam ahead. I recall the drive home vividly as power lines were going down all around me during the 25 mile drive. The roads and fields were scattered with trees and other debris blowing in all directions. It was a gloomy drive with no street lights or building lights along the way and with flashes of lighting in all directions. We both made it home safely in record time as the dangerous storm was headed in the opposite direction of our town. I soon learned at 5 am the next morning, the plant was hit hard, very hard.

I arrived at work before 6 am and Carl had been there for quite a while. An estimated two of four F4 tornados in the area hit the plant right at 11:00 pm. This was only 20 minutes after Mitch and I had left. Thankfully no one was injured at the plant, but we suffered great loss in the area including 11 fatalities in Jackson. The scene that morning was one of devastating damage to the region as well as to the plant. It was a large plant of over 600,000 sf, but only 280,000 sf were being utilized at the time for manufacturing operations. The part of the plant used for manufacturing suffered only minor comparative damage including broken windows, many sections of the roof torn apart, and obviously loss of all utilities. The older, vacant section of the plant suffered more damage which ultimately led to the demolition of over 240,000 sf valued in excess of $5,000,000.

There we were on a Monday morning in the aftermath, as employees faithfully began to show up for work. Many had suffered personal loss; most were in shock, including us, the writers of this traumatic event. Did we have a plan? No. Would one quickly need to evolve to provide our employees a job and our customers their products? You better believe it.

The initial word on that Monday, May 5, 2003, was that we would be without electricity for at least 7-8 days. Throughout that day, the news became more dismal as the true magnitude of the damage in the area became known. The forecast by the end of the day indicated that we would be without power for 12-14 days. How can we possibly run a large manufacturing plant with heavy power factors and demands without electricity for this long? We realized quickly that we could not afford the cost of over 150 employees getting paid to clean up building debris or to cut up blown down trees and fences. Of course, this also had to be done quickly, but it was relatively short-term and wouldn't sustain the majority of our workforce. Still, we were amazed at how the team pulled together and went to work on these items. This had nothing to do with leadership or management; these were good people with genuine compassion and pride for their families at home and at work. I will forever be in debt to the lessons learned from my co-workers at this location. In many ways, they helped raise me.

We quickly took roll call that first day and began to ask about our work families. Many phones calls were coming in and going out to determine the needs and status of our crews. We spent that day focused on each other's needs beyond the immediate needs of the plant. We loaded up crews in trucks with several chain saws and axes as we knew several members had trees down. We quickly learned that several members had trees on their homes, in their living rooms, in their kitchens, and in their bedrooms. It was a very long first day and night in the aftermath, but again, the team stepped up to the plate and did a remarkable job.

The next day, we continued efforts of contacting and checking on other members from the plant as well as their families. Traditional phone lines were down in most of the area, so we either made cell calls or paid visits to homes. A few of our work family did suffer major losses of their homes, cars, and belongings. The municipal organized response groups and volunteers in the area were amazing, but the magnitude of the damage was overwhelming. Those of us who were able and did not suffer extensive loss, quickly put together a list of co-workers and their needs. Clothes, food, supplies, housing arrangements, and manpower were gathered and sent out in teams to assist. It was clear that all were thankful to be alive knowing casualties were suffered in the town. It also became very clear that most were concerned about their job and getting future paychecks.

Carl and I made various phone calls to all the local utilities for updates on service. It was still a bleak forecast of up to 14 days without electricity. The plant was a heavy industrial site utilizing over 8000 amps spread across multiple substations and transformers on the site. We were also a heavy natural gas user. In a ceramic operation, the main furnaces (kilns) are always a major concern in a power failure since prolonged downtime can cause massive product loss. Producing items that require processing temperatures anywhere from 2000-2400 degrees in Fahrenheit in a 24/7 operation, requires a lot of gas. It takes days for the kilns to lose all the heat inside of them. It also takes days to bring the heat back up. We knew one of our first priorities for the plant was to get the kilns operational.

We brought a gas company group in to quickly access the gas lines on the property and inside the plant to ensure no leaks or damage existed. Fortunately, they were fine and passed inspection. Moreover, the gas company assured us that that the main lines were operational and ready to supply. So we had the go ahead for gas but still needed electricity for fan motors and multiple controls.

I started looking at various generator options which were becoming slimmer by the hour. I called my oldest brother, Mark, who ran a manufacturing plant only a few miles down the road. His plant produced automotive parts for Toyota, and I figured that Toyota doesn't wait on parts from anybody for long. Sure enough, he had the plant up and running two days after the storm. I drove to his plant and met him around back. Here sat a very large generator the size of an 18 wheel trailer tied into the main power substation. This generator was large enough that the entire factory was running in all areas! Ok, this was earlier in my career, and since then, I have seen quite a few; but at the time, I was amazed and floored. I called Carl and said, "Git your butt over here to see this thing!" In no time, we both agreed we should locate a generator and get the plant operational for all involved ASAP. I made some phone calls to the contacts Mark provided, and we had our generator on site within a few hours. It took a few more hours to get the Gen-set all wired up, but that night we had power in the plant and started firing the kilns up. All in all, we had the plant back in production and our staff back to work in 72 hours.

Carl-

My tornado experience started with me being awakened before midnight by a horrendous crash outside my bedroom door. I grabbed a flashlight and ran to the living room where I discovered a tree in the middle of the room -a big one. I distinctly remember thinking "hmm, this can't be good." At that moment, my cell phone rang. The shift supervisor told me of the tornado strike and assured me that all personnel on duty were accounted for. Thank God, everyone was safe. I threw on some clothes and headed out the door of my apartment where I saw that every car but mine - 50 or 60 of them - had hail-broken windshields. Yay, I thought, I didn't get hit very hard. Daylight would prove that my car's body work more than made up for the intact windshield, but that's another story. My path to the factory was wide open, and I had no trouble with the drive. *(bg) I must insert here that Carl's car was a POS anyway.*

After checking in with the supervisor and assuring all the employees had left safely, we took a flashlight-lit stroll through the factory. Ceramic factories process dirt and move it around, basically, and the tornado had spread our dirt from one end of the plant to the other. Still, it appeared that the factory was largely intact. Sunrise would prove the damage to be extensive as Bryan has described.

Well before dawn, I left a voice mail for my new boss in Dallas and asked that he call me as soon as possible. I looked forward to his guidance and support as I naturally had a right to expect. He telephoned my cell at about 9 am. It was a short phone call and went something like this:

VP:"How bad is the damage?"

Carl: "It's pretty bad, and the biggest problem is we have no power. The utility company is saying it may be weeks before we will be back up. There are no standing power poles within 2 miles. By the way, no plant personnel were injured, but we don't have full reports on our people who were at home during the strike."

VP: "Well, let us know when you will be back up and running, and let us know if we can help."

Click.

It became <u>abundantly</u> clear that we couldn't expect much corporate help. In later days I would look enviously at the Procter & Gamble food factory next door, that within twenty-four hours of the event, had hundreds of company personnel reporting from distant locations to help their factory management. Just as my call with the VP ended, Bryan walked up to me and told me my former boss, Bill Hanks, had telephoned him to ask how he could help. Bill wasn't even working for the company any longer but had offered to fly up and run a bulldozer if we needed him. The difference between Bill and my new boss was the difference between a leader and someone with little more to offer than a title.

Looking Bryan in the eye I said "Buddy, we are on our own." He replied, simply, "OK, let's rock n' roll." Of course we weren't on our own, but we were without direct corporate help. We didn't waste much phone time subsequently asking them for guidance, either. The team worked together to make good decisions and carry them out.

We were blessed that our corporate insurance was carried by Factory Mutual. Now I'm not here to advise anyone on insurance firms, but one of the most helpful people we worked with during the recovery was Mr. Thomas Pazdera, an adjustor dispatched from St. Louis. Coincidentally, Tom is an alumnus of The

University of Missouri-Rolla, *(now the Missouri University of Science and Technology)* as I am, and I found him to be an absolute, straight shooter regarding what we could and couldn't do under the terms of our policy. He and his team quickly assessed damage, advised us on different options, and generally made my life much easier by helping to show a clear path.

Local and distant contractors showed up by the dozens, and naturally, were profit motivated. Thankfully, the ones we chose to do work for us did the work well and quickly.

Most importantly, our own plant group pulled together as I never thought possible. Bryan has described to you already the actual procedure by which the plant was restored to a functioning state. I will mention also the incredible efforts our entire staff expended to make it happen and the almost heroic deeds that many performed in service to our employees. Groups went to the damaged homes of employees to remove trees from roofs; clothes were delivered to employees' flooded homes. Meals were prepared and delivered by those who had power to those who did not. Employees' homes were opened to those made homeless.

I've often been asked why our employees did these things. Certainly they were not forced or even asked to do them. There was no profit motive in any of their actions, no gain to be had. The answer is simply that this factory was truly the factory family that we have described. Like any family, they might cuss and fuss at each other under normal circumstances but will come together with striking speed in times of tragedy. The way everyone pulled together was both a testament of their innate goodness but indicative of their sense of company as a team with all invested in the welfare of the plant. If there were not this unique culture in the plant, the result could have been employees who reacted as the VP- let us know when to come back to work. And you will be paying us in the meantime ... right?

The management team's motivation for getting the plant back up as quickly as possible was two-fold. First, we wanted to make sure that our customers would suffer minimal disruption to their supply chain. Second, the longer the plant was down, the longer it would be before our people could draw a paycheck. As I look back on the episode, I am pretty sure the second reason was the most important to me. Nobody ever died because their tile shipment was late, but missing a payday can cause major disruption in an employee's life.

It is true that disaster will bring out either the best or worst in people and organizations. Books are written and major motion pictures are filmed to illustrate this phenomenon. It isn't new. Books are written and movies are also filmed in which the long term effects of disaster on people and relationships are described. What Bryan and I learned was that we are well and truly capable of judgment calls that benefit the many; that we aren't afraid of making big decisions; and that we came to be better leaders after facing adversity. You can, too. Keep your heart above your head.

20

Failure IS An Option

In the movie Apollo 13, Ed Harris, playing NASA Flight Director Gene Kranz, yells out to the control room "….failure is not an option!" The movie tagline "Failure is not an option!" has since been used by U.S. Presidents, Senators, Congressmen, and maybe your boss to attach a sense of imperative to goals and plans. Truth is, Kranz never said it. According to Jerry C. Bostick, Flight Dynamics Officer (FDO) Apollo 13: "As far as the expression 'Failure is not an option' … Kranz never used that term … script writers, Al Reinart and Bill Broyles, came down to Clear Lake to interview me on 'what are the people in Mission control really like?' One of their questions was 'Weren't there times when everybody, or at least a few people, just panicked?' My answer was 'No, when bad things happened, we just calmly laid out all the options, and failure was not one of them.' " (http:/spaceacts.com/notanoption.htm) From that interview came a pretty inspiring movie scene. We're pretty sure when all the scientists, engineers, and managers at NASA were scrambling to figure out a way astronauts Jim Lovell, Jack Swigert, and Fred Haise could get back home in their crippled spacecraft that nobody piped up and said "Well, screw it. Those guys are toast!" We're also pretty sure that there were multiple possible solutions devised for each problem - *in case the first one didn't work!*

God bless Ron Howard and Tom Hanks, but yelling out movie taglines is no way to run a government or a factory.

Carl-

If I was going to run around a factory shouting out movie taglines, my favorite would have to be, "I love the smell of napalm in the morning." But that's just me.

Consider the graph below published by the United States Commerce Department in its 2008 Research Report on manufacturing firms from the Center for Economic Studies and Research Data Centers. It clearly shows that after the first year of operation 19.6% of employees' positions will disappear, while 15.4% of those firms that survive will create new jobs. The most telling thing in this chart is how job destruction is greater than job creation until a company is more than 25 years old. Even in these older firms, jobs are still being destroyed; plant closures are quite likely parts of that destruction.

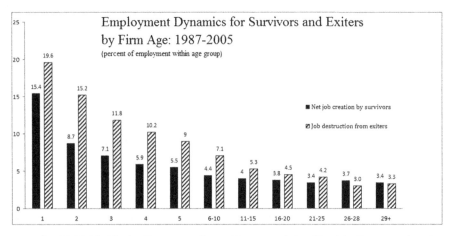

Like NASA's Flight Director Gene Kranz and Apollo 13 Commander Jim Lovell, you will not <u>choose</u> failure as an option, but it may be thrust upon you.

Managing Failure

Success can be relatively easy to manage. If you are in the happy position of being sold out, with customers clamoring for more, you will face challenges. Expansion, hiring, permitting, and all the things associated with increasing production become urgent. These challenges can be large, and naturally you will have to do them uncomfortably and quickly. Expansions can be hard, but the difficulty pales in comparison to the skills needed to manage failures, such as poor plant startup or a factory closure.

You've already learned there are no absolutes of black and white On The Plant Floor, so it will come as no surprise that failure also comes in shades of gray. You will learn more from these failures and become a better manager. However, be prepared for the pain that will come with the education. We will address two serious factory situations – one of which you can influence (plant startup) and one of which you cannot (plant shutdown).

Special Case-The Plant Start-Up

In this case, start-up means Plant #1 for a new company -a new plant, with a new process, in a new location. This is *true* start-up and is also something that we have lived and managed.

A new plant start-up is the polar opposite of a plant closing. As a manager, you will lead the effort, take responsibility for the results, and have the rare opportunity to form a plant culture. Big job? Be prepared to Cowboy Up, partner.

You will start from ground zero. Depending on the size and temperament of your company, you may have a great deal of corporate resources. You may have corporate engineering services, personnel support, regulatory support, and well-defined, corporate polices.

If your company is a true start-up and embarking on manufacturing for the first time you may not have any of these advantages.

Carl –

In the mid-eighties, I had the pleasure of building and starting a new facility for a well-established, manufacturing company. I was able to concentrate on the construction of the physical plant, work flow, and team building because the support function of payroll, environmental permitting, and personnel were handled at the corporate level with minimal input from me. I did not have to worry about office supplies, raw material purchases, credit, and so on. Even though we were starting up a plant making a new ceramic product, it was still a product in the "family" of products in which the company had experience and that had been manufactured for many years in other parts of the world. In short, I was able to concentrate on the things that I felt were important, vital to success, and I let the devil take the hindmost, confident that the technical issues were under control.

Several years later, Bryan and I started up a plant for a company which had never manufactured a single product and was to produce a world-first product. Outside of R&D, we had little support for this endeavor of building a plant without a well-defined product and process on a limited capital budget that, if blown-out, would kill the company.

Well, let me tell you – the differences between the two start-ups were staggering, and it wasn't because I was considerably older this time! Both start-ups were successful, but each required vastly different approaches.

If you are charged with starting up a new operation, understand that failure is an option, but we can offer the following guidance.

- Scope – Ground Zero. Welcome to Gilligan's Island! No phone, no lights, no motor cars, not a single luxury -really! You may well be faced with this in a literal sense. A new facility might not be equipped with an IT network, copying machines, or even pens and pencils. Make an assessment, get the basics, and build from there. Remember that nobody is around to do it for you.

- But it works in the Lab. Riggghhhhhttttt! It works in the lab, but that sure doesn't mean it will work the first time in your brand-spanking new factory. You will fight many battles in a plant start-up, but the battle to convince your R&D team and your top leadership of scale-up issues will be the most important. The only way we know to convince your R&D team that production situations are not directly scalable is data, data, more data. We were once assured by an R&D manager, "I have never failed!" After the failure of his formula we could only make headway in solving the problem by producing reams of reliable data; his personality would not allow him to believe he was fallible. Fortunately, reliable data doesn't have a personality. Ultimately, the infallible R&D manager blamed the problem on "unknowable" unknowns. Fine. Just so long as we could move forward!

- Pilot, pilot, pilot. The concept of a pilot plant, one that provides good upscale, is an absolute must for initial success. A jump from laboratory

ON THE PLANT FLOOR

scale to production scale is one that requires the middle ground of a pilot plant showing the limitations and restrictions in a new process. Established companies recognize this, and start-up companies generally don't. The enthusiasm inherent in start-ups often masks the need for strong, progressive steps toward the end goal. The promise of unimaginable riches, fame and glory will blind all to the reality of a high, manufacturing, failure rate for new companies that transfer technology directly from the lab.

- Build it and they will come. This ain't Kansas, Dorothy, and you aren't carving a baseball field out of a corn patch in Iowa, Ray. No, the promise of a start-up can only be fulfilled if your company has a place to ship product. It is not wrong for manufacturing people to demand an answer to the question of if it has a place to sell product. More companies have failed because of a bad marketing plan than have failed because of manufacturing issues. Where is the Waldo hiding the sales forecast?

- Develop a strong support network. You don't have to be alone, but you will be unless you understand the need for a good network. The start-up experience is so intense that there will be little time to figure it out as you go. You need places to find answers and resources. Strong relationships with your suppliers, the chamber of commerce, and/or economic development groups are likely candidates for the network. Don't forget internal resources, either. The homegrown supervisor you hired to run the gee-gaw press just might be able to lead you in the direction you need to go to find a fabrication shop or a contract welder.

- Have an exit strategy. You may give your heart and soul to the start-up company, make good decisions, and bleed company colors but still not be able to make it work for you. Discontent grows rapidly in this bitter soil, and you will need to recognize the impact on your effectiveness. Be alert to this and understand that the results of the business plan should determine your exit, not your emotions.

In start-up operations, like no other, the principal of "Everything rises and falls on leadership" is paramount. Your leader may have an engaging personality, an advanced degree from a prestigious University, and the ability to charm the snakes into leaving Ireland; but unless his application matches his education (Chapter 22), your road will be long, hard, and filled with frustration.

Start-ups will require you to have an entrepreneurial spirit with high levels of skill and inner resources coupled with a high tolerance for risk. You will need a strong sense of autonomy, self-control, and optimism. If you don't possess these characteristics, you may fail, but you will become more resilient with that failure and be better prepared for what the future will bring. If others around you have not yet had the privilege of failing, _be warned!_ Your experience is critical to the success of the organization, and without it, the firm has a high probability of failure.

Plant Shutdown

There may come a time that despite your teams' best efforts, your improvements and innovations, and your skill at managing upstream, that a high level decision has been made that your location will be closed. We have been there, and unfortunately, done that.

The first thing necessary in managing a closure is your recognition that people will be profoundly affected. They will go through the seven stages of grief (shock, guilt, anger, depression, adjustment, reconstruction, and acceptance), just as if they had lost a loved one. And this makes sense. It's long been recognized that job loss is one of the most traumatic experiences. How much effort (as a percentage of the process) you will have to devote to managing this process depends on several factors.

- Environmental: If your industry has been experiencing shrinkage over a period of years, or your geographical area has suffered a recent history of plant closures, the culture shock can be somewhat tempered. It will still be serious because it is happening to _your_ plant this time.

- Experience: If your plant is mature, peopled by folks who have been employed there since you were a teenager, the sense of loss for your folks can be almost overwhelming.

- Education: Folks who have little education, or those who have worked only at your plant-specific jobs will fear the future more than will your more educated folks. The level of fear is a significant issue with which you will have to deal.

The fear of _what may happen_ by corporate management can lead rational executives to make lousy decisions. If you have ever seen a plant where people come to work one day, handed a check with explanation that the plant is closing and their jobs are gone - leave immediately! - then you have seen scared executives making lousy decisions. In these days of the federal WARN act (Worker Adjustment and Retraining Notification) and attendant state laws, there is, in our opinion and experience, only one reason for an abrupt plant closing – your company is dissolving and has, literally, no way to make payroll.

Unless you are telling your significant other that the jeans they are wearing don't make their butt look big, there is seldom a reason to mislead people. And there is no place for untruths during a plant closure. Can you tell the team and the troops everything? Probably not. Your corporate management will entrust you with information that is best not shared, and a plant closure is not the place to bare your soul. Once a plant closure or significant layoff is announced, the rumor mill at your plant will go into overdrive. When you walk the floor, people who have never said more than "Hey!" to you will ask you very specific questions about severance pay, timing, and general questions as to why the plant is closing, and what they should do when it does. It doesn't matter that you and your company have already outlined what is going to happen; people will want more information than they have been given. Although you will be tempted to help these folks by answering their questions, there is no place for speculation in this process any more than there is a place for dishonesty. Listen to the questions thoughtfully, and note how many people are asking similar questions. If you detect a pattern to the questions you are prohibited from answering, it is in the best interest of all for you to challenge that corporate decision. You know your people better than they do, after all, and, in reality, your corporate personnel department is relying on you to feed them information about your people. Sadly, you will be asked emotional questions like, "How am I supposed to make my rent?" You will really have no answer except, "I just really don't know."

A normal reaction to a plant closing you might have is to let your plant personnel group (HR!) do all the dirty work. This is a bad idea on several levels. If you allow a personnel group to deliver bad news, you will lose any control you have to positively influence the terms of severance for your people. Just as bad, you will serve notice that you are no longer a factor in the chain of command. In the case of a plant cut-back, you will play hell operating the plant at the reduced levels. People just won't trust you. No, cowboy up and be prepared to deliver the bad news with the responsibility your position demands.

A little secret is that all severance benefits are negotiable. For example, your unwritten corporate policy may offer that severance pay, in the case of closure, is one week pay for every year employed. Any plant population can thus be translated to a hard dollar amount. Use that money to tailor distribution to the best advantage for your people. If you have a population with long experience, you can move dollar amounts from those in the lower ranks of service. You might come up with a plan in which those with 20 years of experience receive 30 weeks' severance, while the threshold for any severance pay is two years. The reality is someone in the corporate hierarchy has determined an overall cost of closing your plant. If the number is $3 million and you can eliminate costs from the non-people category by $1 million, you now have $1 million that can be devoted to the benefit of your people. Whether we want to acknowledge it or not, a dollar on a balance sheet is a dollar on the balance sheet, no matter where it is spent. Use your heart and your brain to make it count for your people.

In the case of plant closure and cutback, the government is your friend. Really! It is a sign of the times that most states have well-developed groups that aid in educating and helping your affected people to get access to extended, unemployment benefits, free education benefits, job re-training, and health insurance benefits. These services are _FREE_ to the company and employee. Like all government programs, it is incumbent on the employer to properly apply for them. Do not rely on your personnel people (HR!) to fully understand and take care of this. We have seen companies in which affected people lose out on needed, government benefits due to the ineptitude of personnel departments coupled with presumptions by plant management. Two good resources are:

Trade Adjustment Act (TAA) http://www.loleta.gove/tradeact/

Rapid Response Services: http://www.doleta.gov/layoff/rapid.cfm

Plant cutback and closure is a process just like (except for the pain) any other manufacturing process. And like any other process, you will need a plan that includes both corporate and local objectives which are measurable and achievable. Although you may be past the point of arguing against the plant closure, you are not past the point where you are able to help define the objectives of the plant closure and resulting benefit to your people.

There is another shock of which you need to be aware - the shock to you. Do not think that because you have advance knowledge of the corporate action and you're ready to "cowboy up" that you will not be affected. The reality of a plant closure is that you will suffer symptoms similar to PTSD (Post Traumatic Stress Disorder). It will not matter if you have opportunities at another company location, whether you are close to retirement and will receive a significant severance benefit, or are so disgusted by the situation that you are ready to leave anyway. You are going to go through significant times during this closure that can bring significant personal problems. We are not psychologists, just a couple of guys who have gone through it, but we know that you will have to deal with your personal issues in order to control your emotions during this process. Be aware, and be prepared to deal with the stress.

Every night for 4 months after the plant closed, I was the last person to leave. I led a small closure team of 10 co-workers who were tasked with removing all the equipment from the plant by auction, relocation to another plant, or to be scrapped. Our role was to empty the building so that it would be more attractive for resale. We now were removing the equipment that we spent years trying to keep running. It was a large plant and each night I walked the floors and aisles going to each station to turn the lights out and lock all the doors. It was deathly quiet and lonely. No machines running, no forklift traffic, no pages from the loud speaker, no compressor noise or pipes rattling, no large electrical panels buzzing, or products moving all through the operation. And the worst part of it all, none of the many people I had worked with for almost 20 years. I found myself sitting in the floor many nights in tears for belief of ultimate, personal cause and failure by not being able to do something that prevented the inevitable closure. The life of a plant manager at the time of a closure is vast emptiness. I vowed to never be involved with one again. - Bryan

Failure and You

Unless you are in a tiny minority, you will not end your career working for only one employer. Like most of us, you will work for multiple firms - perhaps in multiple locations. Does changing jobs mean you are a failure? After all, if your plant closes and you are forced to find another job, it means you failed, right? What if you are recruited by another firm with a substantial, salary increase? That means you are a success, right? How on earth can you be a either a success or a failure with the _identical_ outcomes of going to a new job?

The lesson of failure is in how you deal with it. Your success depends not on failed operations or promotions, but in how well you learn the lesson.

"I never failed once.
It just happened to be a 2000-step process."
-Thomas Edison

21

In Or Out Of the Organization

Making a Choice Beyond Economics

As we write this in late 2010, the official national unemployment rate has just hit 9.8%, rising from 4.6% in 2007. Obviously a lot of people have been forced to change jobs in the past three years, and a very great many have not yet found gainful employment. Arguments over the best way out of underemployment will continue to rage in Government quarters, and ideological battles will be fought twenty-four hours a day on Fox, CNN, and MSNBC. While your humble authors certainly have political views and will be more than happy to engage in ideological battles, we are concerned in this chapter with that which is missed in this debate - even in the worst employment economy since the early '80's, people continue to leave jobs *by their own choice*.

If you are one of the unemployed, you may well say to yourself that once you find a new job, you will never quit and will retire from that company. *(Carl —Yep. I've certainly said that!)* The odds of that coming to pass are against you, and not because the company fails. According to the Bureau of Labor Statistics, the median tenure in a job is 4.8 years in this admittedly bad economy. But the same BLS statistics show that current tenures have risen only slightly from 4.4 years in the best employment years. This 0.4 year difference only amounts to about six months. We can see, then, that many people are going to have around eight to ten jobs in their working career. Heck, if you assume that even half (a very generous estimate) of those job changes are because you will get fired or downsized, you will still end up leaving *by your own choice* four or five times in your career.

People leave jobs for all kinds of reasons, and we are not here to judge the validity of those reasons if they are external. After all, sometimes stuff just happens. You might have to leave a job because your spouse hates the location. You might have to quit because your aging parents back in Ohio need your help. You may quit because you win a lottery! Who really knows what can happen in your personal life that will affect your continued employment? Your authors surely don't, so we will not be so arrogant as to tell you if they are good reasons or not. Still, be aware of external factors and understand they *will* be a factor in any decision you make.

Our book has largely talked about your role as a team member and as a leader. However, the decision to leave your job or stay is intensely personal. This is not a chapter about the management methods used to reduce turnover in your factory – it is about how to recognize and deal with your own particular situation and whether *you* will be in or out of the organization.

Despite all the disclaimers on employment applications, reminding you that your employment is "at will," and "employment does not imply contractual obligation;" all employment is basically a contract between you and your employer. (We will assume here that as a management employee, you are not covered by any bargaining agreement.) The contract is: you show up for work and perform your job duties, and the company will pay you an agreed amount on a regular basis. Really simple, right? Well, you know that there is much more to it. Your boss and employer are evaluating you on a regular basis, and you are evaluating them as well. And this will be true in every job you have. Remember, we all have bosses even if we own our own company (the customer). The happy situation is when this constant scrutiny on both sides leads to the mutually, satisfactory conclusion in which both you and your employer are happy with the contract. In this case, all is well and good - continue to do your best, work hard, and take a few tips from this book. Nobody is happier for you than us.

If you are still reading this chapter, you have probably done some evaluation of your company and found it wanting. If you are faced with deciding your place in or out of the organization, read on.

In The Organization

Many problems with the workplace contract can be solved, but they won't be unless your boss and your company know your objectives don't align with theirs. Yep, here it is again - communication. If you keep your concerns to yourself, then don't be surprised if your boss seems unsympathetic – he can't read minds. Before you go off half-cocked and air a laundry list to your boss or the personnel department, stop and consider the following:

- Is it reasonable? If you expect a plant manager's salary for a first line supervision position, then you're probably in for disappointment. Asking your boss the best way to get to the next level is reasonable.

- Is the problem me? As a human being you might make an all too human mistake and assign fault to your company instead of realizing you are the problem. If you are bored and unchallenged, desiring a change, take good stock of yourself. You might be the problem. Zig Ziglar once said: "A lot of people quit looking for work when they find a job." In these days of increasing workload and job sharing, it may be hard to believe that people are unchallenged, but it does happen. *Carl – I once hired a young engineer recently graduated from a prestigious school in the great state of Georgia. After training him for six months, by rotating him through different factory sequences, I assigned him responsibility for the quality control function of the entire plant. After about 3 months, during which he made little, forward progress improving recovery and reducing customer complaints, he came to me and let me know he was bored and working too many hours. He believed the QC job was beneath his abilities and wanted to do something else. We discussed his problem for well over an hour; I closed the meeting with a word of advice to him: "Jim, I think you need to find something to do outside the company and outside of manufacturing. We have talked many times about your lack of progress. It would be one thing if you had come to me and were bored because you fixed all our problems and are ready to hand the QC function off to someone else. It is quite another to come in and complain about boredom and long hours when you have nothing to show for three months of being in charge. Go home and think about it." He resigned soon after to take a job with another factory only to be fired in four months. The last I heard, he was teaching high school in Georgia. I may have made a mistake in hiring him, but the problem with his employment was his to solve, not ours. He was lazy and not suited to the factory life.*

• Is your problem temporary? We've heard it said: "Act in haste and repent in leisure," and it certainly applies in evaluating your company. Start-ups of any kind can bring a lot of frustration and take time to smooth out. Is your problem like a start-up that is likely to lessen over time? If you determine it is, ride it out.

• Is your company headed up or down? Looking for solutions to your problems, especially if they involve money, is going to be a difficult sale if your company is missing financial targets.

• Is the problem internal or external? We often think our job is the problem when outside factors are where our discomfort is truly felt. Your company can't solve personal issues, but they may be willing to help through employee counseling services that are commonly available these days.

Once you consider these issues, you are ready to communicate the problem. No matter what the issue is, go to your boss first – even if the problem is with him. You owe him that, and he will be in the best position to represent you and help in solving the problem. There may be a natural tendency to avoid confrontation if your problem is with him, but don't bypass him. Communications of this type are always best handled in person, but that's unrealistic if your boss is a thousand miles away. As tempting as it might be, don't send the evil, flaming email! Use the phone. As tactfully as you can, explain the problem his behavior is causing you in doing your job. He may not agree with you, but you might just get him to thinking about his actions. And in the event he is just a total jerk, all you will do in bypassing him is enrage him. Either way, you lose.

One final thought on communication for supervisors and managers: Don't burst in your boss's office letting him know that if he doesn't fix your problem, you are going to quit. Once you threaten to quit, you have already quit. The only question left is how soon you are going to leave the building.

Out of the Organization-It's time to go

There may come a time in your career when no communication is going to fix a problem; no amount of hard work will solve an issue, and there is no other path except to find your place out of the organization. We know this because we have been there.

- When you come to understand that your company's leadership and culture are not aligned with your own, it's time to go.

- When you find yourself standing against your leadership in continual argument because you don't believe their directives will work, it's time to go.

- When you find yourself not caring whether the right things are done, it's time to go.

- When you find yourself dreading routine meetings and phone calls from your superiors, it's time to go.

- When you loathe each and every workday – no matter what is scheduled, it's time to go.

- When you are slowly disintegrating from the stress, and you secretly pray for deliverance, it's time to go

- When you find no humor in life, it's time to go.

What you have lost is *belief*. You've lost belief in your company; you've lost belief in your ability to influence events; you've lost belief in yourself as a leader. Once your situation leads you to lose these core professional beliefs, your _only_ solution is to leave the company. Active belief in your organization is essential for leaders and managers. As we have pointed out, be genuine and people will know it; fake it, and they will know it as well. And isn't belief a very hard thing for most people to fake? If your situation is fixable when you still believe, the economics of remaining in your job will play a large part in your decision to stay or go - at least it will until you find another position. But if you have lost your belief, the decision to leave goes far beyond economics.

Our phrase "beyond economics" can be explained with a simple question: Does the risk of an uncertain future outweigh the hell you are in now? Only you can answer the question. Really, it is a personal decision that must be made with your immediate family. Others in your life have no relevant input. Your father, brother, pastor, uncle, and close friends are important to you, but they aren't the ones who will suffer or prosper from their well-meaning advice. We aren't telling you to quit a bad job or to stay in it. We are telling you that it's likely you will face a decision beyond economics – in or out of the organization. That may be today, tomorrow, or in ten years, but it will come. Your authors faced this situation, and we can tell you that there is life beyond economics.

Trying to hang onto a paycheck in a crisis of belief will diminish you. Just as importantly, it will diminish those around you – both on the job and at home. The decision to leave must be about who you are and what you believe in. In the final analysis people will not remember you for your position; they will remember what you were.

"I am tomorrow, or some future day, what I establish today. I am today what I established yesterday or some previous day."- James Joyce

22

Education vs. Application

Equipping The Plant Supervisor

Despite the gloom and doom headlines of constant factory closings, manufacturing is alive and well in the US and offering rewarding employment. The definition of manufacturing today cannot be considered as simply turning raw materials into finished goods. With technological advancements in production equipment, sophisticated inventory control, and real-time supply chain management, today's modern manufacturing plant requires talent *with* skills. A good example in our career deals with the firing of ceramic tiles. 20+ years ago, the standard method involved tunnel kilns sintering the tiles up to 2200F requiring 24 to 48 hrs in the kiln. Today, tiles are fired in roller hearth kilns at the same temperature in less than 40 minutes. That's right, from cold-to-hot-to-cold is less than 40 minutes compared to a few years ago requiring up to 2 days.

The manual workforce has been replaced in all areas possible to reduce labor cost, improve efficiency, and increase outputs. Complex control systems, lean manufacturing, and six sigma are prominent on the plant floors. Digital and robotic factories can be found all across our great country. These advancements demand that managers and supervisors be much more than overseers or baby-sitters. Progressive and constant training along with hiring really smart people are a must. Do you find yourself interviewing more candidates for each job than ever before? Yes. Does this mean that the qualifications should always require a degree or advanced degree to manage on the plant floor? That's what we will cover here: the need to find a balance of education vs. application as well as how to equip managers for battle.

Members of a previous team that we formed reported that new leader-ship stated that all supervisors going forward would need to be engineers. The team obviously was concerned since most of the existing managers were not engineers. Should all supervisors on the plant floor be engineers? The vote would be pretty split depending on the group questioned. Want to know our thoughts? It should be split. Forming a balance of technical skills, theory, and science with those that are experienced and seasoned in manufacturing is a winning formula. Hiring all engineers and expecting them to excel, lead, and deal with the complex personalities in a manufacturing plant can be a disaster. If your recent hire is from the university of "I just graduated summa cum laude," and you immediately put them over a sequence in the plant, what are their chances for success? If you hire someone from another manufactur-ing plant that has +10 yrs experience supervising on the plant floor and no degree, what are their chances for success? What is the success rate if you put the two together? These are obviously loaded questions that depend much on the individual. However, the destiny of the team, regardless of their education level, goes higher up the command chain. Once again – everything rides on the plant leadership.

The Hiring Gamble

Ken Iverson was known as a business maverick and has an astonishing track record of success, which includes building Nucor from ground zero to an empire. In the epilogue of Mr. Iverson's book *"Plain Talk,"* he talks about the pos-sible cure for the common MBA. He points out his learning curve of forming teams made up of MBAs hired out of the top business schools. *"They've come to us, degree in hand, and ready to conquer the world. We soon found out they couldn't conquer the basics of managing a department."*

The ultimate quest of hiring new employees always involves much more than compromising just to fill a role or position. Ever compromise on hiring? Sure, we all have, but never underestimate how news spreads about the leaders in a plant. Especially bad news. Let's hope this is not the case, and people are knocking on your door because of the positive buzz in town about your leadership style. Let's consider we are looking for a plant supervisor. We'll look at the requirements as True or False.

- Degree required? (Let's leave open for now.)

- High intelligence? TRUE

- Experience required? (We could leave open but rarely will you actually hire someone for supervisory position without experience.) How much? At least 5 yrs. TRUE

- Works well with others? Of course, TRUE

- Excellent communication skills? TRUE

- Excellent organizational skills? TRUE

- Safety knowledge including OHSA? TRUE

- Problem-solving skills? TRUE

- Talent? TRUE

- Passion? TRUE

- Teachable? TRUE

- Strong work ethic? TRUE

This list could continue but covers 90% of the general requirements when looking for potential candidates. Some are easily identified through their resume, experiences, and the interviewing process. Others, such as talent and passion, require a deeper dive, such as checking professional and personal references.

Notice all the obvious TRUE questions that most of us would agree are essential for a supervisor. Do all of these requirements automatically equal TRUE if the candidate has a degree? Do all of these requirements automatically equal false if the candidate does not have a degree? The argument could be that if you can find a degreed contender with the experience and the other requirements, are they preferred? Perhaps, but what assures you of their passion, ability to learn, and work ethic anymore than the non-degreed?

Discovering someone's talent and passion empowers you to value what they do naturally well, and what they enjoy doing. Do they have a passion for manufacturing? Are they comfortable in this environment? A manager or supervisor in the plant has to be well-rounded and sharp – very sharp. Strong technical skills, people skills, and leadership skills are the heartbeat of a supervisor. Hiring someone that has adequate training for the job but lacks talent and driving passion will often yield to mediocre and disengaged managers on the plant floor. Are their expectations to work on spreadsheets, charts, and statistics all day in the office? These are vital requirements in today's manufacturing plant, but it will not be the majority of their day. Perhaps you have dedicated engineering positions for these functions and more, which is great, but are they also production supervisors? It still boils down to a balanced group of managers and leaders in the manufacturing plants. No doubt you can have two equally educated and trained professionals working in the same job and produce completely different results in terms of performance and value added. Talent, passion, and work ethic may very well separate the ones that excel from the ones that fail.

Promoting From Within

As we addressed right off the bat in "Welcome To Management," we fully support promoting from within. This speaks volumes for a leadership group that recognizes talent, passion, and proven results inside the ranks. Of course, care has to be taken to safeguard that the desire to promote someone matches the new role, or you potentially promote failure. Not to belabor the topic, but leadership has failed when a new supervisor falls short. This is especially the case when you promote someone from within, as adequate time has been allowed by you and your peers to make certain the promotion is a win-win for the plant and individual.

More often than not, promoting someone from within the manufacturing plant will include operators or technicians. On average, these candidates will not have a college degree. Do you have a program that would assist them in returning to school or seeking continued education? Encourage this in a way that does not belittle or intimidate them, but offers an avenue to improve their knowledge and skills that will further assist them and the plant. Whether it's back to school, classes in the plant, or some other form of training, we should all agree that when you are done learning – you are done.

The Apprentice

Developing a strong team of plant supervisors goes beyond forming a strategic balance of education and application. Whether a new supervisor has a master's degree or high school diploma, the plant leadership and culture will need to foster their development. A superb start for a new supervisor is to spend as much time as possible with veteran supervisors. The veteran supervisor should have a teaching spirit and zeal for wanting to share his experience with others. Of course, there will be a period to digest "junior, "rookie," "grasshopper" and so on, but this will pass depending on how fast the student catches on. Again we stress, finding the right senior supervisor to give lessons is key as this is not the time for a hazing or tearing down. It's time to build a firm foundation grounded in the virtues of the plant culture that include respect, engagement, disclosure, integrity, and humility.

We consider this period of apprenticeship not optional. The absolute future of the institution hangs on your ability to develop new talent and leadership. Will today's supervisors be tomorrow's operation managers, plant managers, vice presidents, or presidents? Why not? So spend the time equipping them with the needed tools for success such as a mentor. If you have multiple mentors in the plant, allow each of them to work with the new supervisor. This gives the new supervisor numerous methods on how to handle various situations. Expect a few failures along the way, this builds character and humbles hot shots. Lessons learned are lessons earned.

Don't be too proud to take lessons. I'm not. – Jack Nicklaus

Many of these situations we have covered in this work, so feel free to utilize this book and get the new supervisor a copy.

Start-up Teams

If you are building a new plant, doing an expansion, or starting up new equipment, the value of a well-balanced team will shine – or fade quickly if out of balance. On a recent job we were on for several months, there were quite a few challenges. New technologies, new processes, and a new product- new to the world, and required much adaptation. As always, there were money and livelihoods at stake, and at times, tensions were wound very tight. We had a great team (the best), and one of the most experienced supervisors kept a phrase very active during this time: "It's just manufacturing." And so it was and they all persevered, kept their chins up, and executed like the true champions they are. Now, if the team had not been well-balanced with experienced leaders (most non-degreed) and a strong technical staff (most well-degreed), managing the concerns and uncertainties would have been overwhelming. Our seasoned supervisors worked through the equipment installations, start-ups, and modifications just as they had many others times in their careers. Their "it's just manufacturing" mentality never grew weary from the long hours, constant time on the floor, and relentless engagement with vendors. Sometimes the relations with vendors were very taxing and required strong forceful demands to guarantee a win. They never waivered; it was natural and instinctive. These experienced leaders managed the situations at hand while the technical staff in the lab was able to continue their focus on testing needs, quality control parameters, and standard operating procedures. Communication was high and support between the groups created dynamic synergy. They all had diverse backgrounds and various levels of education but pulled the rope in the same direction while showing mutual respect for their roles.

Attitude

Attitude has almost become politically incorrect in that it typically suggests that someone is "bad". As you know well by now, being politically correct is not one of our strong points, so we will discuss attitude as we see it. Attitude is something you can't hardly dumb down or educate up. Bad attitudes are easy to identify as they surface frequently from those carrying them. How do we identify and enhance great attitudes? It's not about being smart enough. As we have mentioned, you want to make sure to hire very intelligent people, degreed or not. But a great IQ does not equal a great attitude. Attitude is discernible, and here are some metrics that gage it's condition. Consider the opposites as warning signs.

- Speech: provides upbeat, optimistic, and encouraging dialogue and feedback.

- Change: is a change agent, supports others changes, and remains flexible.

- Takes responsibility: can fall on their own sword and does not shift the blame.

- Adapts and overcomes: maintains a no-quit mind set.

- Not lazy: well educated or not, laziness is a cardinal sin.

Attitude is really who you are. *In spite of your education level, talent, skill, and passion, attitude can be the main breaker switch that turns the rest of the power off.* Attitude can either stifle or let out your real potential.

There are zillions of self-help guides and 21 day steps to a more positive attitude. But how can we build great or improved attitudes in the plant? Many things shape a person's attitude before they ever reach the manufacturing plant environment. This is another reason it is critical to get the right people on the bus before telling the driver to head up the mountain. Nevertheless, the plant culture and leadership can cast and mold attitude into the shape needed by what others see and hear around them. Talk about how screwed up the company is, clueless your boss is, and send the message that we're all going to die = kills attitude. Lead in a manner that consistently shows respect, loyalty, and the ability to overcome failures = saves attitude.

Equipping the new supervisor with the best armor for battle requires commitment from those on the plant floor. We do not agree with requiring all the plant leaders to have college degrees or to be engineers, but we strongly support education. Forming a balanced team of experienced leaders with the "it's just manufacturing" mentality and working side by side with new supervisors improves your overall plant culture. Seeking, developing, and sustaining talent, passion, work ethic, and great attitude will ensure that the education meets the application.

23

Staying Humble

Looking In The Mirror

For centuries, it has been debated on what characteristics and skills define a great leader. Those of us who have realized the need to improve our skills and the ultimate responsibility to others for our actions, continue to look in the mirror. We accept that self-examination is not for vanity but in humble recognition of our duty to serve as well as to lead.

Talent is God given. Be humble. Fame is man-given. Be grateful. Conceit is self-given. Be careful. – John Wooden

Most of us have learned humility the hard way through personal and professional failure. How does the road to humility apply to the manufacturing plant arena? It allows leaders and team members to understand and accept strengths and weaknesses. Acknowledging weaknesses creates great opportunity to grow as managers or supervisors. If key positions stop growing, then the plant stops growing as well. As you grow, so grows your team and co-workers; as they grow, so grows the institution. Staying humble can be learned, as mentioned, through failures. It also can be taught by example, sometimes even if it is unknown to the teacher.

During one of our journeys to locate an area to build a manufacturing plant, we were blessed to locate someone locally that had a profound effect on our success. More so, he had a lifelong impact on us personally. During our site selection process, we traveled across 22 states, met with countless local and state officials, and reviewed over 80 pieces of potential properties. This tour required over 8 months of resolve and eventually led us back to an area we had looked at months earlier. Here is where we met William. He was in an unfortunate position of being left in charge to manage the closure of a local factory in the community. Like us, he had been in manufacturing for many years, and to be involved with a closure was taking the wind out of his sails. It took us no time to appreciate Will as a humble giant and someone we wanted on our team. He became our first hire for the new operation. Being in the area all of his life, Will added tremendous value to our team with access to local resources, other talent to hire (or not), and the ability to hit the ground running. From day 1, Will picked up a broom during the construction process, made dozens of trips on his own for local supplies, assisted with engineering, managed installations, and even cleaned the restrooms. Will was a very hard worker, super smart, and our go-to guy. As we began to interview and hire others, Will became the benchmark. Often, we would say, "If you cannot get along with Will, take a look in the mirror." We did not meet anyone that Will could not work with or could not encourage to do a better job. While some of us fight many inner battles that struggle with physical and mental warfare, it was obvious that Will had won the ultimate battle. He had spiritual control of his life, and it showed each day through his humility. Having just come through a plant closure, Will was thrilled to be on the other side of the fence to build something from scratch, have a voice in the design, and to be able to create jobs instead of eliminate them. He helped us to form the culture we set out to do, which included respect to all, engagement, disclosure, integrity, compassion, and humility. Thank you, William, for the many lessons.

Staying humble is one of the leadership traits that you do not see as frequently as you should. Some will consider it a weakness and feel that being humble means letting others run over you. This is not the case at all. It does, however,

170

keep your position of power from clouding your judgment. If you are constantly making others *feel less than you*, you need to work on humility. Staying humble is much easier when you yield to the fact that no one person has all the answers.

Bryan —

I have yet to make a change or decision on my own in a plant that was as well thought- out and productive as those made by discussing with my team first.

Adding Value

Sharing your experiences and wisdom is critical in developing others. This requires dedication, patience, and willingness. Consider this conversation between your two authors.

"Bryan, how much time do you spend each day adding value to others?"

"Not near enough."

"Well, that's not good. What are we gonna do about it?"

"Carl, I'm not sure. You know, I work day and night on about 40 different things at any giving time. I'm no cry baby, but if we fail to execute something quick in some of these areas, we're headed downhill fast. Plus, I have talked to the team until I am blue in the face about what needs to be done. At this point, how can I work on adding value to others?"

"Bryan, I have told you time and time again to let me help in some areas or delegate some things to others. The company and plant will suffer much more if you do not spend time maintaining the basic values needed for the plant culture."

"You know what Carl, you're right. At the end of the day, if we don't sustain the culture, the other 40 things won't matter. Here's what I'm thinking of starting immediately: I don't have all the answers and will look for opportunities to learn something new from others. I will also attempt to help in areas that I can with what skills I've gained. I am going to be mindful to share my experience and wisdom, but in a way that no one should ever feel 'less than me'. Let me hear your thoughts on these daily changes."

1. The first hour of every day will be spent talking to the night shift supervisors to *ensure* that they have the support needed. I also want to encourage them by *thanking* them for their service and hard work. I want them to leave feeling good about the plant leadership, and to know without a doubt that I *believe* in them and their teams. I also want their crews to know how I *appreciate* their significant contributions, and I will show *compassion* to those working the night shift hours required.

2. During that first hour of each day I will get to *engage* the next crew as they come in and start their shift. A simple good morning with a smile

and asking "how are you?" might go a long way at getting their day off to a nice start. I also want to make sure that they see me listening to their supervisor and showing *respect* to his decisions.

3. While I am making the rounds to get the day started, I want to be sure that I stop by the maintenance shop and the lab. These two support groups are essential to the plant's success, and I always *learn* a great deal from them. They typically have a few questions about the company outlook, so I want to make sure I *disclose* any details that I can to them.

4. A couple of times a week, I will take supervisors (one or two at a time) from the plant out to lunch. Getting them away from the plant for a short time is a good change. Also, they will see that I have a *genuine* interest in them, and that I am grateful for their dedication to the plant.

5. Each day, I will talk to members in each sequence in a manner that shows my humility toward their help in producing the top quality products we need for our customers.

"So what do you think, Carl?"

"Bryan, what is described here are the core values that will serve you and this group well for many years to come."

✓ Becoming a better listener

✓ Asking questions in a nonthreatening way

✓ Equipping (making sure others have the tools they need to succeed)

✓ Mentoring

✓ Working on relationships

Infecting others with your passion

Showing your humility (giving credit to others for the plant's victories)

Have Charisma But Remain Humble

Charismatic people draw others to them with their personality. Their innate ability to interface in a personal and direct manner allows them to effectively communicate and persuade others. They can take command of an audience by inspiring and motivating others with their energy. Sometimes it can be hard to put your finger on why charismatic people are so magnetic, but this ability allows them to form relationships and lead others. They most often possess great communication skills, including their ability to listen well to others and create synergies from their feedback. There is possibly no better way to draw people to you than to be known as a humble person.

Examples of well-known charismatic leaders include: Winston Churchill, Abraham Lincoln, Ronald Reagan, Billy Graham, Charles Manson, and Adolf Hitler. As you can see, the list contains both constructive and destructive leaders who all had the ability to convince others to do extraordinary things, good and bad. In this section we are addressing how charisma can be a great tool for communicating effectively, while making strong interpersonal connections, as well as maintaining your humility in the process.

Advantages From Developing Constructive Charisma:

- Adoration without effort

- Self-confidence and self-esteem are improved

- You possess authority without being intimidating

- Others feel comfortable around you

- Others want to instinctively follow and assist you

Whether you are running a corporation, a manufacturing plant, a sequence, a classroom, or attempting to run your household, these advantages are ones we all need. Unlocking your potential to positively influence others will absolutely get more done in a shorter time. As we say quite often, getting everyone to pull the rope in the same direction is one of the toughest challenges a leader will face day in and day out. Here are some tips to developing or improving your charisma.

- *Smile* (This seems so simple yet is so hard for many to do as they apparently believe that always having a disappointed look gets more done.)

- *Show interest* (As we mentioned in *You Manage Things — You Lead People,* everyone has a story to tell. Be genuine and remain teachable – everyone can still learn something.)

173

- *Be all there* (Pay attention, look them in the eye, and avoid distractions when listening to others. Remember people's names as this proves your attention and retention.)

- *Show confidence* (This includes being self-confident and having confidence in others. Self-confidence includes being assertive, but not to the point of haughtiness that slaps humility in the face.

- *Improve speaking* (The power of persuasion is very limited without effective speaking skills. Your enthusiasm and passion can be felt in your voice as well as your actions.)

Perhaps charisma is 50% born with traits and 50% developed as many are still trying to figure out the mystery of how some have it and some don't. In any case, most of us agree that charisma is a good attribute to have in a leader who has a friendly personality and drive that friends and strangers want to be around. Be charismatic so that others will follow your lead, but remain humble so that they keep following.

Give It Away

I don't know what your destiny will be, but one thing I know: The only ones among you who will be really happy are those who have sought and found how to serve.
-Albert Schweitzer

Never lose sight that regardless of the workload, stress, and challenges faced as a leader in the plant, it is an honor. You are one of the few that make the decisions that form the culture of the operation. Your service speaks for the company, the plant, and the employees- to the customer.

Making the change from taking the credit for accomplishments to giving the success to others comes with experience. Insecurities and a need to justify one's existence cause many to constantly use terms such as "I" and "Me." As you grow, terms such as "We" and "They" begin to take precedence as you give the credit away. This requires maintaining a *Servant's Heart*. Do not label the term servant to those at lower levels or at the bottom of the totem pole. It's more about attitude than position. You are consistently able to put others needs above your own. This goes many directions, meaning the sacrifice for the company, for the plant, and for the plant personnel. You work toward recognition and rewards for others to allow them to grow under your command. You go to bat for them time and again in areas of promotion and salary. Wait ... did you just say get them more money? We sure did. It is one of your great responsibilities to take care of your team and their families by making sure they are rewarded for their dedication and service. This is never something for nothing. As you have read all through this work, we believe in pushing hard, setting high expectations, and holding others (as well as ourselves) very accountable. When it's time and all is justified, you need to push for more money for your team.

Your ability to stay humble, serve, and give credit to others for the plant's success will be a large part of the culture and legacy that you leave. Being around humble people is refreshing. Arrogance grows old fast.

24

The Balance

Ouch! This subject area still hurts each time we bring it up. How many of us have struggled with finding a good balance between life inside the plant and life outside the plant? Ok, you can all put your hands down now. As a manager, the amount of dedication and sacrifice required on the plant floor can be massive. There will be numerous times when your responsibilities at the plant require many, many hours. You will work multiple shifts and weekends and get called in with little sleep. You will cancel personal engagements, vacations, and miss your childs' ball games. Your obligations at the plant will cause added tension at home. Your spouse and children will, in turn, share in your sacrifice to the plant.

Now, after reading that opening paragraph, some of you are nodding your head in total agreement, and others are shaking it off as -not me. If you are fully engaged in the operation and have accepted more and more responsibility over time, you know the sacrifice. If you are new to management and the factory life, soon you will be nodding in agreement or finding a new career. It's simply a reality of life in a manufacturing operation that runs 24/7. It is really that bad? At times, worse, and other times, much better. The key is to know when your presence and assistance is required, and when it is not. A large part of the balance falls solely upon _your_ shoulders.

How can you, as a leader, expect others to be so dedicated, focused, and unwavering, if you are not working as many or more hours than anyone else? There is a question that rings true in several of our minds. Is it really about the hours and time at the plant or the results? If I can get done what is needed in 8 hrs, isn't that enough? Yes and no.

When you come right down to it, if you are going to establish as part of the plant culture, "do not abandon ship or leave an area in chaos," plan to stay too. Here you might say something such as, "I'm not a mechanic, electrician, or quality control person that adds real value, so why should I stay?" Again, remember the culture, the engagement, full disclosure, managing upstream and downstream, spreading the pain, and finally, "Cowboy Up!" Show the troops that your commitment to the cause is substantial, and avoid hypocrisy. Let them see you on the battle field with them, fighting for the cause.

That said, plant manager: you are ultimately responsible for your plant and your staff, which includes your team's ability to find the balance. There are days, nights, and shifts when you should stay and/or have others stay the course and see the issue through. There are many times when you are called outside of work that you should go in and get involved. Then there are times also, when you should lead in another direction. The balance is a partnership. You, the plant manager, have the other set of shoulders that help determine which way the balance tilts.

We were blessed with a lab staff at one location that was unmatched in dedication, performance, and constant positive results. They are second to none in our manufacturing experience across several locations over the years. This group was relatively inexperienced in a manufacturing environment. They moved hundreds of miles away from their families to be a part of a colossal challenge. They took the bull by both horns and held on for dear life. We constantly had to step in and say, "Ok, shut 'er down; it's time to go home." Sometimes they listened; sometimes they did not, until we put a boot in their behinds. We had to enforce things such as taking vacation days, not working every weekend, reducing their hours, and at times, not getting involved with every event within the plant. Did we appreciate this group? Did they add tremendous value to the plant? Did they help meet an unbelievable schedule involving start-up? More so, did they help develop the type of culture we needed for the plant? Absolutely! Without a doubt they were engaged at a level that spoke volumes for our core belief system and promoted it to all involved. Yet we were ultimately responsible for helping to develop a balance for them that they would pass on to others for many years. They placed enormous faith in us.

In this context, faith could be referred to as the opposite of worry. Worry can, in fact, strangle and choke the life out of faith. Make sure others are not often discouraged or constantly stressed over the battles at work adding to tension at home. Step in and help clarify the balance when needed. Showing faith in them to manage their sequence requires that they show faith in their crew as well. Leaving work and then calling every hour to see how things are going shows great dedication, but it also shows lack of confidence in your staff. In return, if they feel they must constantly call you, or you instructed them to do so, it shows little faith in them. Set conditions for calls. Safety issues such as injuries, equipment down for x amount of time, and major quality problems are some of the examples. Make sure the staff knows they can call you anytime (be accessible) but faithfully expect them to manage most situations.

A few chapters ago, we discussed "Spreading The Pain" and how to rotate supervision, maintenance, and other support groups to areas that are lagging. This ensures that a certain sequence or few select groups are not suffering the load of the plant. In that same chapter, we introduced you to *Entitlements* that can play a critical role if particular individuals or sequences are hitting brick walls and not showing progress. Once again, bringing in support from others can promote improvements, while keeping a sequence and supervisor from being out of balance. Letting others know this expectation is a part of the plant culture reduces any thoughts that seeking help is a weakness. We have yet to see a company, plant, or sequence excel at a greater pace than a group pulling in the same direction, instead of only one set of hands on the rope. Those hands alone will get very sore and very tired. They will eventually let go, lose their balance, and fall. Recognize as a leader, if they fall, it was on your watch.

As you know all too well in management, many eyes are upon you. Some anxiously await your lead—including what time they can go home. Have you developed a culture that says no one can leave until the boss does? Some will answer, "No, but I'm not a babysitter, and others have to make their own decisions." Fair enough. But have you told your staff they do NOT have to wait until you leave? Here are a few specific examples on do's and don'ts.

- The plant manager is staying late to work on a budget update required for the corporate office. Two other managers are staying late also, because they do not want to leave before the boss. Their areas are running well, and they should leave. Instead, they stay at their offices and catch up on war stories, or possibly gripe about how many hours they put in. Why? Honestly, fear of being considered a slacker or part-timer. Truth: it's a waste of plant time and personal time. At fault: a poorly defined culture for the plant that creates constant insecurity.

- Line 3 has a furnace down, and the supervisor is working with the maintenance staff to resolve. The problem has been pinpointed, and parts are being replaced. It is late in the evening, and the plant manager is still there as well. He's dedicated and wants to see the furnace back up and running before leaving. This is great, but the supervisor has already informed the plant manager that the line will be running in a few hours, and that he will stay with it. The plant manager remains in his office, surfing the internet, until the furnace is running. Again, it's a waste of plant time and personal time that erodes at a balance.

- It is 6:00 pm on Friday evening, and the day shift managers are wrapping it up. There is a page over the loud speaker for maintenance to mixer 2. The managers leave. At 10:00 pm the mixer supervisor gets a call from the off-shift supervisor stating mixer 2 has been down since 6:00 pm with no remedy in sight. In this example, 2 of the managers that left, the mixer supervisor and the maintenance manager, should have checked on the problem when they heard the page. Now both are called into work after 10:00pm on a Friday night.

It should be obvious that we could not give these types of specific examples unless we had lived them. We have and often times allowed a poor balance for ourselves and others. We could not have written this chapter 10 years ago -maybe even 5 years ago. We learned the hard way and have begun to accept the responsibility as key leaders for a better balance. This comes with experience (yes age) and developing a more genuine care for life outside the plant for yourself as well as for others. It does not mean you are forming a culture of slack or less dedication, or that it is acceptable to miss goals. There will be 80-100 hour weeks that require all troops to be boots on the ground. Start-ups, equipment installations, expansions, and God forbid natural disasters, are all good examples of these times. There are many other weeks when 50-60 hours gets the job done. We do not say 40 hours and there is a reason.

If 40 hours a week maintains a smooth and effective operation, 10 more hours per week can easily be dedicated to events that sustain the culture needed. More examples:

- Helping another sequence and manager that is struggling

- Catching up on reports and email instead of sitting in front of a laptop at home each night (again this does not mean wasting time at work surfing the net ... more on this later)

- Training and coaching others

- Get on the plant floor. Be visible talking to the plant staff, including other managers, maintenance, the lab, and operators. Know their names, their roles, and their history with the plant. Talk about work and life away from work. Do not forget to also thank them for their service.

This seems basic and easy. Spending 1 or 2 hours a day just walking around and talking to people, helping others, encouraging, training? Yep, easy, and how many actually get it done? Ok, only a few hands went up that time.

We have mentioned surfing the net at work a couple of times already in this chapter. It is impossible to function in today's world without the internet. Global access to all that is involved in a plant is critical, or we take serious steps backward in productivity. Data tracking, research, order status, customer feedback, emails, and so on is a daily requirement. However, wasting time shopping, taking care of personal emails, looking for another job, and on and on is one of the worst, bad habits in business. Most companies have provisional software that monitors, prevents, and establishes boundaries for the internet. Still, many do not, and believe that in good faith employees will do their job. Years ago, it might be someone simply spending too much time playing solitaire at their desk. We all know too well with the technology advancements of computers and faster internet, we are way beyond solitaire.

It should be policy concerning not wasting time (whether considered on or off the clock) on the internet with non-work related events. Put it in the handbook, lead by example, and remind others in staff meetings of your stance in this area.

These are obviously common sense approaches to maintaining a balance in the plant, but how often do we fail? You have heard us say a few times already that *everything rises and falls on leadership.** A large part of the fall involves losing your balance. Time on and off the playing field are required, and the coach typically calls in the players from the field. Again, we emphasize to the leaders in the plant; your responsibility includes a balance. Don't burn your players out, or you risk failures on multiple levels. These can include turn-over, injuries, and a reduced passion for excellence. We all get tired, we all get frustrated, and we all need time off. There will be times the coach has to step in and bench some players for rest. Do it.

Several years ago when asked how many hours I worked in a week, the answer might be in a proud and honorable voice, "It is nothing for me to work 80-100 hours per week. I love my job, the company, my staff; it's my responsibility to be there." I would often get a response from others about how tough that must be and asked how does your family feel about it and so on. The standard answer was always how they understood what was required and the level of dedication needed. Did they really? Sometimes yes and many times, no. Is it proud and honorable to boast of this level of commitment to the plant? Of course it can be, but for who? It is certainly not for the family that you missed every dinner with this week. Did you have to do it, or did you justify it as your job? Sometimes yes and many times, no. Again, we (the authors) have the battle scars to show you. Lessons earned should yield lessons learned.

We truly believe that all the chapters in this work are critical and provide valuable assistance to the manufacturing group. But similar to a great record album, some songs are enjoyed more than others. Our hope is that you find this chapter to be one that you listen to over and over again. It will take considerable self-examination, as well as exceptionable leadership, to form the balance needed to ensure you and your team are successful on and off the plant floor. Remind yourself often that the balance largely depends upon two sets of shoulders, your own and your boss's.

* John C. Maxwell

25

The Final Product

Making A Difference

We have covered a lot of ground with "On The Plant Floor," and the closing chapter will wrap it all up as the final product. The manufacturing plant team is similar to an orchestra. Every musician is an artist in his or her own right. It's only when they play together that the problems might develop. The plant leadership is charged with being expert problem solvers and the ultimate conductor, so that the music continues to flow as it should in harmony. At the heart of this book is our sincere goal to offer frontline techniques in the plant that encourages others by promoting excellence through leadership.

Try to touch someone's heart before you ask for their hand. — John C. Maxwell

Mentoring is a definitive way to add value to people. It becomes all about the other person and your ability to give in a way that encourages, develops, corrects, and guides. Focus on the person and not just the work that needs to be done. Don't attempt to pass on traits to others that you do not possess. Again, be real since ego must take a backseat as you realize the fragileness of someone else that is under your wing. To help determine who you should mentor, use the 80/20 rule. Spend 80% of your time developing the top 20% around you. Realize that some are not ready to be mentored, and others simply do not want to be. Invest in those who will give the greatest return. Do not take on those who simply want to be closer to or get in good with the boss. During mentoring, you will have to find the balance between praising them and raising them. At times, you must be firm, but also, *Trust* them.

T rust

E ncourage

A ssist

C oach

H elp

Generosity is not only measured in dollars, but in how much of yourself you give away. *You can make a difference in others.*

Regardless of your title in the plant, you will play many roles at various times and stages during your career. Whether you are a supervisor, manager, coach, counselor, or mentor, employees all call for you to be a leader. People have to believe in you before they will believe in your leadership. Creating *genuine* belief in each other requires that in *Building The Culture,* you lay a firm foundation. The cornerstone of this foundation is grounded in a *mutual respect* to each member of the plant despite their position or rank. We cannot stress enough how vital the plant culture is to your individual progress as well as the progress of the entire plant. *You can make a different in the culture.*

This book not only represents our years of experience but also our time of reflection. Looking back at victories and losses, we fully appreciate much more the value of each. The natural fall of man proves that we are prone to failure. The learning experiences from failures certainly promote positive change as they are often very painful. Leading on the plant floor requires that you make constant decisions. Do not fret over failures or bad decisions as they are the ultimate trainers. We think decisions break out into thirds.

✓ 1/3 of your decisions = positive results

✓ 1/3 of your decisions = failure

✓ 1/3 of your decisions = neutral

Waiting on perfect solutions is like waiting on the government. You lose way too much time and speculate over what ifs instead of putting realistic plans into action. *You can make a difference even in failure.*

Self-discipline is a must. This, in fact, may be the greatest struggle in life -period. As you know very well by now, we are not philosophers, but rather, practical guys who admit mistakes and try to keep others from doing the same. Self-discipline is a constant battle on and off the plant floor. It is the one area, perhaps more than any other, which truly leads others by example. Never underestimate your ability from a leadership role to influence others – constructively or destructively. If you are telling others to engage or improve in areas that you cannot yourself, you are part of the problem. If you have a lot of talent, a great team, and put a lot of hard work into action but still lack solid results, you may lack self-discipline.

Self-discipline goes hand in hand with *character*. Abraham Lincoln spoke on character quite often. One speech stated, *"Reputation is the shadow. Character is the tree."* You will encounter many people who will not want to hear what defines character, but it is being real. Be genuine, and it will show; be fake, and it will show also.

Whoso boasteth himself of a false gift is like clouds and wind without rain. – Proverbs 25:14

Our character is not just what we try to display for others to see; it is who we are even when no one is watching. Good character is doing the right thing because it is right to do what is right. Character builds trust in followers. If followers see breaks in character, you become the hypocrite preacher that eventually gets voted out. People lose faith in you. It is hard to imagine a self-improvement plan that does not involve improving character. *You can make a difference in yourself.*

We will mention here, again, the importance of having a *strong #1 and strong #2* in the plant. *Loyalty* between the two must be rock solid. The #1 cannot operate in fear that the #2 is out to take his job. The #2 cannot operate in a manner that is to undermine and slash the throat of the #1. These two positions will take the most responsibility for the overall plant performance, and they should lean on each other firmly. *Unity* must be shown on the plant floor from these two positions, or the foundation has flaws, and the building could fall. Your two authors worked this way for many years and found each time that the whole was always greater than the sum of its parts. *We made a difference in each other.*

As students and teachers, we often ask this question, "Why do some who reach a leadership position never acknowledge the need to improve their own leadership skills?" Most of the time it is not a matter of being so arrogant that they feel like they have all the answers. It is simply hard to find the time needed for personal development. And frankly, most companies today do not invest the time and capital into developing their employees further. So, is it easier to deal with constant turnover and to blame inadequate performers for all of the plant's problems? Certainly not, and if you have matured in your position much at all, you understand that your team's failures represent your management and leadership flaws. Leadership is influence, positive or negative. Do you go to bat for your team by attempting to get more training? Are you in a position that you could very well budget for this and you don't? *Are you making a difference?*

Does personal improvement in the plant only come with age and experience? While time is perhaps the greatest teacher of all, the sooner you accept the need to improve in many areas, the sooner you will get busy at it. If you suffer from thinking you are the smartest guy in the room, be prepared to have all the *correct* answers. Also, be prepared to have more failures than others as it may take multiple setbacks to turn you. Perfection is not required. Potential and work ethic are. The path to becoming a better leader starts with the individual. All the training in the world from the best mentors you can find cannot force someone to improve their own weaknesses. We all have to reach a point in life where we accept the honor and duty entitled to us by being able to lead and manage for the company and your team. For some, this will come earlier than with others. *You can make a difference at any age.*

What is your legacy to the plant and to its people? Being on the plant floor is our belief system because the action in manufacturing is, in fact, *on the plant floor.*

It is the grand arena that you should love and fill at home in when you are there. Just as others show their pride to announce their profession as a doctor, lawyer, or college professor, you will be just as proud to state that you make things for a living. Supervisors, other managers, and especially the hourly workers should consider your presence on the plant floor as normal. If every time a team member sees you on the plant floor, and their reaction is, "Oh crap, what's wrong now?"- you should spend a lot more time on the plant floor. Be fully engaged in your operation by knowing the process at expert level and knowing your team's strengths and weaknesses. This will allow you to continue to work on areas of improvements, such as training needs, equipment/engineering needs, housekeeping needs, and constantly keeping the orchestra in tune. If it's in your blood, manufacturing is your livelihood; do not be casual about it. Work closely with your team to learn and grow with each other as well as the operation. *You can make a difference on the plant floor.*

On The Plant Floor

Made in the USA
Columbia, SC
08 August 2020